Landmark
B O O K S

ALEXANDER HAMILTON
AND AARON BURR
Their Lives, Their Times, Their Duel

Alexander Hamilton and Aaron Burr

Their Lives, Their Times, Their Duel

BY ANNA ERSKINE CROUSE

AND RUSSEL CROUSE

ILLUSTRATED BY WALTER BUEHR

RANDOM HOUSE · NEW YORK

Contents

ALEXANDER HAMILTON
AND AARON BURR
Their Lives, Their Times, Their Duel

Prologue

As the sun broke through the early morning haze on July 11, 1804, a rowboat, its oars muffled, made its way across the Hudson River from New York to the shore of New Jersey at a point called Weehawken.

Two men stepped ashore and climbed the rocks to a narrow ledge above. They looked about, then started removing branches of trees and bushes to make a clearing for the duel. They stopped as they heard the oars of another boat. Soon two more men were climbing the rocks.

As they reached the ledge they nodded silently to the others. Two of the men met, the duelists' seconds, and talked a moment. A coin was tossed. They looked at it, then each rejoined his companion. A box was produced and opened. It held two pistols which gleamed as they caught the sunlight.

Slowly one of the men measured ten paces. He turned to the two duelists and nodded. They took their places at either end of the paced clearing. Each now took a pistol and held it by his side.

"Are you ready?" asked the man who stood to one side halfway between them.

"Yes," they answered.

There was a moment of silence.

"Present!" said the man.

A shot broke the silence sharply. One of the men rose on his toes. His arm went up. His pistol fired, the shot going into the branches of a tree overhead. He swerved slightly and fell, face forward. The other stepped toward him, as if he wished he could undo what he had done. His second caught his sleeve— and then hurried him away.

Thus ended the most famous duel in American history. The next day Alexander Hamilton was dead, the victim of the shot fired by Aaron Burr. That shot had ended the life of a great statesman and had ended, too, the career of one who might have been just as great.

What had happened to lead to this tragedy?

· 1 ·

To
America

It is strange but true that many of America's early heroes were not Americans at all. The country was too young to produce all its leaders.

So it was with Alexander Hamilton. He was born on the lazy little British island of Nevis in the Caribbean Sea on January 11, 1755. In those days the islands of the West Indies, of which Nevis was one, were a haven for many who sought either freedom or fortune.

Alexander's heritage combined both. His mother's father, John Faucette, a Huguenot, had fled France and settled on Nevis so that he could worship as he pleased. His father, James Hamilton, was of fine Scottish stock, the son of the Laird of Cambuskeith, who had come to the West Indies to seek his fortune.

Alexander grew up in Charlestown, the capital of the island. It was a rich community because of the island's valuable crop, sugar, but his family didn't share these riches. His father was a failure in business.

Alexander was a bright boy—small, red-headed, handsome, alert. He listened and he learned. He heard many stories of the world outside Nevis and longed to see it.

"How would you like to take a journey?" his father said to him one day.

Alexander's heart leaped.

"Where?" he asked, holding his breath.

"To St. Croix," his father replied.

St. Croix! An island almost next door! Alexander was disappointed. But it was travel and his father had to go. He had found work with a firm which sent him there. Alexander moved with his father and mother and older brother to Christiansted. But the Hamilton fortunes were no better there. Finally, discouraged and conscience-stricken at his failure, James went to Rachel, Alexander's mother, and told her he was going away alone. She and her boys never saw him again.

But if his father had no head for business, Alexander's mother did. She had set up a shop (in their home) where she sold food and household articles, most of which she bought from a firm of young merchants, David Beekman and Nicholas Cruger, who imported them. She did well enough to support her sons.

Alexander's older cousin, Peter Lytton, kept books for her, but it wasn't his regular job so he couldn't always be on hand. Alexander was a diligent and good student. One day Peter saw him at his homework. He watched him a few minutes.

"Alex," he said in admiration, "you're quite a hand at figures."

"I like them," the boy replied.

"I'll teach you to keep accounts," his cousin said. He did, and quickly, for Alexander was already showing some of the mathematical genius that was later to make him America's greatest financial guiding hand. He was so good at keeping his mother's books that Nicholas Cruger turned over his company's accounts to him, too.

Young Alex, his reddish hair in a tight pigtail, saw much in Cruger's shop and office. Out the window he would watch the harbor—pirate ships and merchant vessels moored side by side. On the streets were swashbuckling buccaneers, some with scars and eye patches, and good, sound sea captains with shiny, hard hats, and sailors in striped shorts and stocking caps.

The shop dealt in mules, lumber, rum, molasses, cotton and sugar, the sweet source of wealth on the island. It dealt in slaves, too—Negro men, women and children brought ashore from boats just in from Africa, pitiful figures shaking with fright, tearful with homesickness and still in chains.

Alexander made excellent progress in Cruger's shop. Then when he was only thirteen came a great blow. One morning in February, 1768, his mother awoke with a high fever.

"What'll we do?" asked Jimmy of his brother Alex.

"Let's ask Mistress MacDonnell," said the frightened Alex.

Ann MacDonnell was a lodger in their home. They ran to her.

"No need for a doctor," said Mistress MacDonnell. "I'll take care of her."

Rachel grew worse. Mistress MacDonnell finally called a barber, who "bled" her. This was a common practice in those days—to take blood from a patient. In some cases it was effective but in this case it was the greatest error that could have been made. A few days later, Rachel was dead.

The two boys were orphans.

Jimmy had been apprenticed to a carpenter, who took him into his home. Nicholas Cruger, now very fond of his young clerk, put his arms around Alex's shoulder.

"Boy," he said with hearty kindliness, "we're both bachelors, you and I."

Alex tried to smile.

"There's plenty of room where I live—you know, up above the shop. How would you like to move up there with me?"

Alex shook hands with him in silent appreciation.

From his desk, young Alex watched the lively harbor.

He was to spend the rest of his days on St. Croix in these new lodgings.

But there was another blow to come. Alex's best friend, Neddy Stevens, was sent to college—King's

College, in New York. Alex was desperately lonesome. He was just as desperately ambitious, too. He wanted to get out into the world—the world that sent its ships into Christiansted harbor.

"My ambition is prevalent," he wrote to Neddy, "so that I contemn the grovelling condition of a clerk or the life to which my fortune condemns me, and would willingly risk my life, though not my character, to exalt my station. . . . I shall conclude by saying I wish there were a war."

Alex didn't really mean it the way it sounds. He was poor and war was his only hope of travel.

But if Alex had lost a friend he also had gained one. For about this time the Reverend Hugh Knox, a Presbyterian minister, arrived in Christiansted. Alex was drawn to him immediately, attracted by his fine liberal mind.

He was just what a boy of sixteen needed—someone with whom to discuss the many things that were on his mind. Knox guided him through many subjects, loaned him many books; and within a year young Hamilton was brilliant beyond his years, and his knowledge was tempered with understanding.

One afternoon in 1772, the clouds grew dark over

Christiansted. The wind's weird wailing increased and finally darkness and disaster fell. It was a hurricane—perhaps the worst in the history of the Indies, the birthplace of hurricanes. It ripped. It tore. And when morning came not a boat remained in the harbor; half the houses in the port were in ruins. Plantations were devastated. Many people were dead.

A few days later the Reverend Mr. Knox dropped in to visit young Alex. He found him writing a letter to his father, who now lived on the island of St. Vincent. It was a letter describing the great storm.

Alex asked him to read what he had written. Knox did. In fact, he could not put it down until he had finished.

"May I have this published?" he said at last.

Alex hesitated.

"But it is magnificent," said Knox.

And so it was published in the *Royal Gazette*. It created a sensation—this vivid, dramatic account of what had just happened to St. Croix. And by a coincidence there appeared in the same issue of the *Gazette* a letter from the Reverend John Witherspoon, president of Princeton College, New Jersey, asking that the sons of the islanders be sent there to be educated.

The hurricane devastated the port of Christiansted.

This was the spark. The Reverend Mr. Knox knew Princeton College. He had studied there. He knew what college would do for Alex. In fact, all St. Croix recognized the brilliance of the story of the hurricane. Princeton was just the place for the boy.

Knox himself helped raise the money for the project. Alex's aunt helped. Nicholas Cruger wrote letters to his family and friends in New York. Knox wrote to friends in Princeton.

In midsummer, 1773, Alexander Hamilton sailed on one of Mr. Cruger's ships. He landed in Boston. But Boston wasn't his destination. He took the first stagecoach to New York.

Hercules Mulligan, a business friend of Mr. Cruger, met him in New York. It wasn't the gay, big city then. Both Boston and Philadelphia were larger. But Alex wasn't concerned with that.

"How do I get to Princeton College?" was what he asked Mr. Mulligan.

• 2 •

College
at 13

The college which Alexander Hamilton hoped to attend was situated in a small community called Prince Town. Surrounded by good farming land and fine forests, Prince Town was the halfway station for the stagecoach between New York and Philadelphia. The College itself consisted of two buildings, Nassau Hall and the President's House. The man who had picked the location and raised the money to move the College of New Jersey to Prince Town seventeen years before was the Reverend Aaron Burr. Later the college was to take its name from the town and become Princeton.

The Reverend Mr. Burr was an intelligent and respected minister, the descendant of a distinguished family in the early history of the American colonies. His great-grandfather, John Burr, had come to this country with Winthrop's fleet in 1630 and had helped in the settling of Springfield, Massachusetts. Things had gone well for the Burrs in this new country and the Reverend Mr. Burr's father was a wealthy land-owner in Fairfield, Connecticut.

This young minister had been graduated from Yale at nineteen with highest honors. He started his career as pastor of the First Presbyterian Church in Newark. He became the second president of the College of New Jersey—a most imposing title, considering that the College consisted of eight pupils who gathered at the parsonage every day for the study of English and the classical languages.

However, the Reverend Mr. Burr dreamed of a really great college, something to rival Yale and Harvard in New England, Kings College in New York, and William and Mary in Virginia. As his classes grew so did his dream. He set about making it a reality.

His wife, Esther Burr, was not only attractive and charming but she was also capable and suited to this life, for she was the daughter of the most famous preacher and teacher of the time, the Reverend Jonathan Edwards. Fifteen years younger than her husband, she somehow managed to be pastor's wife and college president's wife, to bring up her little daughter Sally, keep house, and put up with students in her living room, all at the same time.

The Reverend Mr. Burr spent more and more time traveling as he toured the countryside lecturing and begging for his beloved college. He was determined to raise the money to move his students to a fine new building. During one of his many trips away from home his son was born. The date was February 6, 1756, and Esther named the baby Aaron for his father.

When little Aaron was ten months old the family moved to their new home. Esther was in raptures over the buildings. She wrote a friend: "The college is a fabulous building I assure you and the most commodious of any of the colleges as well as much the largest of any upon the continent." "The largest of any upon the continent" could hold one hundred students.

Esther's happiness was not only in the growth of the college but also in her family. She wrote lovingly of how Sally was growing and said of her baby, "Aaron is a little dirty noisy boy very different from Sally almost in everything. He begins to talk a little, is very sly and mischievous. He has more sprightliness than Sally and most say he is handsomer, but not so good tempered. He is very resolute and requires a good governor to bring him to terms."

Unfortunately, the happiness was not to last. President Burr was not strong, and he had exhausted himself in his work for the college. He became ill with a fever, but would not stop his work. He took the stagecoach to Philadelphia on business. When he returned, still sick, he found that Governor Belcher of New Jersey, a dear friend and patron of the college, had died suddenly. It was a great shock. However, against all advice he insisted on going to Elizabeth and preaching at the funeral. It was too much for him.

He did reach home, but all Esther's loving care could not save him. He died on September 24, 1757.

Esther was heartbroken. She took comfort in her religion and her children. But more tragedy lay ahead. Her father, Jonathan Edwards, was called to take over the presidency of the college. A smallpox epidemic was raging. In March of 1758 he caught the disease and died. One month later Esther came down with the same disease. She too died.

Sally, aged four, and Aaron, aged two, were hurriedly sent to a friend's home in Philadelphia. There they were to await their grandmother, Mrs. Edwards, who would take them under her care. On the journey from the north she became ill, and two weeks after she reached them she died.

So little Aaron, the boy whose mother knew he needed a "good governor," had lost his father, grandfather, mother and grandmother all in one year.

Aaron and Sally were taken in by their uncle, Timothy Edwards, a minister, too. Unfortunately, he had inherited all of his father's puritanical strictness, but none of his understanding and charm. His household was entirely without joy.

"There is but one mode of family government," he

told a friend. "Beware how you let the first act of disobedience in your little boys go unnoticed and unpunished."

Gay, fun-loving, mischievous little Aaron did not go unnoticed! He became quite familiar with his uncle's rod.

It did not take long for Aaron to rebel. At four he ran away, and wasn't found for three days. At ten, he tried again. He fled Elizabethtown and struck out for the shipyards. He found a captain who needed a cabin boy and wasn't particular about his age. Aaron signed on, stowed his small bundle of possessions in his bunk and prepared to see the world. Unfortunately the wind died down, the captain had to await another tide, and Timothy Edwards had time to trace his high-spirited nephew to the ship.

Young Aaron, seeing his uncle stride down the wharf, leaped for the mainmast and climbed to the top with incredible speed.

From this vantage point he bargained with his uncle, who, terrified for his nephew's safety, agreed that if he would return peacefully, he would not be punished.

This escape frightened Timothy Edwards and he

High on the mainmast, Aaron bargained with his uncle.

never again had much control over Aaron. He must have sensed that this was no usual child and certainly his fine rules of government hadn't worked in this case.

Aaron knew his uncle was honestly trying to do what he believed best for his ward. But Burr's adventuresome spirit could not stand the repressions of that home. Running away had not succeeded, but there was a way to free himself to which his uncle could not object. He would get to college as fast as possible.

Timothy Edwards had supplied good tutors for his family and Burr was a bright and willing student. He worked hard to prepare himself for the college. At eleven, he felt he was ready. He presented himself to Dr. Witherspoon, the president of the college. The good man looked with astonishment at the slender boy with the piercing black eyes.

"How do you expect to enter the College of New Jersey at your age?" he asked. "Do you know the requirements?"

"I do, sir," said Burr, "and I would like to be examined."

Dr. Witherspoon examined him carefully and found him well taught in all the required subjects. But he shook his head as he looked at the child. Burr was short for his age and probably appeared even younger than eleven.

"Come back in a few years, boy, and we will be proud to have you."

For the third time, Aaron had to return to Timothy Edwards, but now he had a goal in view and he stayed out of mischief and concentrated on his studies.

At thirteen he returned and reminded Dr. Wither-spoon of his promise. This time he was accepted and that fall he entered the college. His studies had put him so far ahead that he joined the Sophomore class.

The boy whose mother had said he needed a "good governor" was out in the world on his own at thirteen.

• 3 •

The

Restless Colonies

The road to Princeton wasn't as smooth as Alexander Hamilton had expected. Mr. Knox's friends, who welcomed him, decided he needed more schooling before college. They enrolled him in the Francis Barber Grammar School at Elizabethtown, New Jersey.

Alexander worked hard but found time, too, to learn about his new country. He listened eagerly to political discussions in the homes of Elias Boudinot

and William Livingston, his sponsors in Elizabethtown. There was something in the air here in America
—a new sort of feeling for freedom and justice and—
well, a new sort of life. Alex was eager to become a
part of it.

When his year's grammar schooling was over, Alex
took his examinations for Princeton. He passed them,
too. Everyone was pleased, including Dr. Witherspoon. But Alex was in a hurry. He insisted that if he
entered Princeton he be allowed "to advance from
class to class with as much rapidity as his exertions
would enable him to do."

This was something that had to be approved by
the college's trustees. They lost no time in saying no.
And Alex lost no time making new plans. He set out
immediately for New York where his old friend, Ned
Stevens, was a student at King's College. There the
trustees accepted his ambitious proposition. So in
1774 Alex started in college.

The New York into which Alexander Hamilton
moved as a young student was little more than a
village. It barely covered the lower tip of Manhattan
Island and was a maze of crooked, untidy streets.

King's College was a part of this downtown scene

—an unimpressive institution. It had a faculty of three —a professor of anatomy, a professor of chemistry, and its president, Dr. Myles Cooper, who taught Latin, English, Greek, mathematics and philosophy. Today this same college has a faculty of three thousand, and is one of America's great institutions of learning—Columbia University.

Young Hamilton plunged into his studies. Soon he wanted more. He became a private pupil of Dr. Robert Harper in mathematics, a subject that was to mean a great deal to him and to our country one day.

But even his studies were not enough. He and a group of fellow students formed a club for "mutual improvement." Soon it was more than that. Its young members were debating among themselves, making speeches to each other.

Debate was in the air in America. England's hand upon the colonies was becoming heavier and heavier. Many protested the growing tyranny. Others were loyal to their homeland in spite of everything. King's College was in the hands of these loyalists, or Tories, but its students felt no such ties. Theirs was the urge for freedom.

The tax burdens of the colonists grew, and all

these tax laws were made in faraway England without the people in this country having a word to say about them. The mutterings about "taxation without representation" could be heard everywhere.

Then came the match for the powder keg—a tax on tea sent to the colonies. A ship with tea arrived in Boston harbor in December, 1773. On the night of December 16th, a band of citizens disguised as Indians, even to war paint and carrying tomahawks, swarmed aboard the ship and dumped the contents of 342 chests of tea overboard.

New York almost had its own "tea party" shortly afterward. All the colonies seethed with the spirit of revolt. Young Alex and his companions found it hard to debate now for they were all on one side.

Came summer and the interest grew. On a hot July afternoon a great meeting was held in "The Fields" where the town's Liberty Pole stood. The oratory was fiery, the resolutions bold. Young Hamilton stood watching, his lips moving with the speech he wanted to make.

A man alongside him saw this, urged him to mount the platform. His fellow students took up the cry.

"Go ahead, Alex," said Ned Stevens and pushed him up the few steps.

Alex found himself facing the crowd. There was laughter at the sight of the boy. He started, then stopped in a stammer, but began again. This time he kept going. The crowd listened, then cheered. The day's newspapers did not record what he said that July afternoon, but Alexander Hamilton had entered public life—and was never again to be really out of it.

It is difficult to tell just when the Revolution began. There was revolt before shots were fired. Today this early stage would be called "cold war." In this cold war young Hamilton's weapon was his pen.

The first Continental Congress met in Philadelphia in September, 1774. It was a heated but orderly session and did not really take a stand for the "independence" of the colonies—but for their "liberty."

Tories immediately rose to England's defense. One of these was the learned Reverend Samuel Seabury, who published a pamphlet of attack on the Continental Congress, an appeal to farmers.

Shortly thereafter there appeared an answering

pamphlet, sharp and brilliant. Seabury answered back
in print. So did the anonymous defender, with such
skill that all thirteen colonies speculated as to what
"elder statesman" was responsible. Leaders of the
liberty movement found it difficult to believe the au-
thor was a nineteen-year-old college student, Alexander Hamilton.

But the time was rapidly coming for other weap-
ons. All over America men were cleaning their muskets, storing powder and ball. Boston was under
martial law. Trouble was in the air.

Young Hamilton and his friends at King's College
began to get ready for the inevitable. Every morning
before their classes they gathered in the churchyard
of St. George's Chapel to drill. They called themselves the "Corsicans" and wore small rakish round
hats and short green jackets with red hearts inscribed,
"God and Our Right."

The fury of both the Colonials and the British was
mounting, but neither wanted to strike first.

Then on the night of April 18, 1775, the British decided to stop the storing of guns and powder by the
"rebels." A detachment was sent to Concord, Massa-

chusetts. Paul Revere and William Dawes were waiting for a signal of an attack—lanterns to be hung
from Old North Church, "One if by land, two if by
sea."

Every morning the students drilled in the churchyard.

When the two lanterns appeared, Revere and
Dawes rode on to warn the countryside. Next day at
Lexington, then Concord, the first shots were fired
and the Revolution was on in earnest.

In New York City there was rioting. Mobs hunted down Tories. The town was ablaze with rebellion. No one was more fired with the spirit of liberty than young Hamilton, but already he had, also, a strong sense of justice and law and order.

One night in May, 1775, Hamilton was awakened by a sound that couldn't be mistaken—the frightening muffled roar of a mob on the march. He wakened his roommate, Robert Troup, and they dressed hastily and rushed out.

"What's this?" Alex asked one of the rioters.

The man held up a bucket filled with hot tar and pointed to the man next to him carrying a bag of feathers.

"We're going to get that old Tory Cooper," another shouted.

Cooper was the president of Alex's college. There was no doubt that he was a Tory. But he was a human being, too, and as such, in Hamilton's fair mind, deserved the protection of the law.

"Quick!" he whispered to Troup. "Follow me!"

The two took a short cut to Dr. Cooper's house. The leaders of the mob were almost there. Alex leaped to the porch and held up his hand.

"Stop!" he shouted. The leaders halted. They recognized the young man who had addressed them in "The Fields."

"Wait!" he went on. "Think! This isn't liberty. This isn't justice. If you harm Dr. Cooper you will be harming the cause for which you are fighting."

There were voices from the crowd.

"Get out of the way!" shouted one.

"No, he's right," shouted another.

Hamilton took advantage of the dissension and pleaded with them again for justice.

Old Dr. Cooper, wakened by the noise, stuck his head out an upper window. He saw only a speaker addressing a mob.

"Don't listen to him, men," he shouted out the window. "He's crazy!"

The crowd laughed. Its hot-headed drive was thrown off balance. Alex ran to the back door, got Dr. Cooper, guided him to the home of a friend. The mob a moment later was storming through the Tory's house but did not find him.

Hamilton and his companions, the Corsicans, continued to drill. There was open fighting now. General George Washington had been named by the second Continental Congress as commander of the 17,000 Colonial soldiers.

New York's own congress had decided to form a company of artillery. This was Hamilton's chance. He had been studying gunnery diligently. He had no experience but he had friends—men who knew his zeal and his keen mind. He was appointed captain of the "company," but there was as yet no company.

Hamilton himself raised his own little army—sixty-eight men. He used what little money he had to help equip them. Their first duty was to guard the colony's records. It was an actionless task—but not for long.

On July 4, 1776, the Continental Congress, meeting in Philadelphia, adopted a stirring resolution which was to go down in history as the blueprint of liberty —the Declaration of Independence.

A week later the British fleet sailed up the narrows and into New York harbor. General William Howe, with orders to crush the rebellion without delay, made ready to land his army of 34,000 men.

Captain Alexander Hamilton ordered his men to their guns. His college now was secondary. His first thoughts were of the fight for independence which had begun in earnest. The Revolution was soon to claim the attention of Burr, too.

· 4 ·

Off

to Find

a War

Aaron Burr's college career at Princeton was uneventful. The first year he worked too hard. He was anxious to overcome his youth and make certain he kept up with his class. After a summer's rest he returned the next fall determined to mix study with pleasure. He joined the Cleosophic, a debating society, which was about the only activity for students outside of studies and chapel.

Burr's classmates were a serious and intelligent group of boys. Some, like Matthias Ogden, were to remain his steadfast friends for life. Others, like James Madison, were to turn against him and bring on his political downfall. But all were to become distinguished Americans. Future generals, Supreme Court justices, ministers, lawyers and one future President of the United States were among the graduating class of 1772.

Burr stayed on at Princeton for another year. He was only sixteen, still small for his age, precocious, handsome, and attracting friends wherever he went. The time was coming, however, when he would have to make plans for his future.

There had never been any doubt in the minds of his relatives as to Aaron's future career. Since he was the son, grandson and nephew of preachers, it was taken for granted that he would study for the ministry. Burr was not sure but he was willing to give it a try. He chose as his teacher Dr. Joseph Bellamy of Bethlehem, Connecticut, a pupil of his grandfather. For nine months he tried to follow the path of Presbyterianism, but religion was for him a personal matter and not something that followed a strict set of rules. He argued brilliantly with Dr. Bellamy. He already had a lawyer's talent for gathering facts and putting them to their best use. It became obvious that poor Dr. Bellamy was losing the battle—and the pupil. In the summer of 1774, Aaron Burr gave up all thought of becoming a minister.

There were two careers considered proper for young men in those days—the ministry and the law. Having given up the first, Aaron decided to try the second. He wrote Timothy Edwards, asking his advice as to teachers. The old man was now thoroughly discouraged with his ward.

"It is a matter of indifference to me," he wrote. "I would have you act your pleasure therein."

By now he knew his nephew would "act his pleasure" anyway!

Burr chose to study with Tapping Reeve, a fine lawyer who had married Sally Burr. He moved to Litchfield where the Reeves lived.

This was the summer of 1774. Oddly enough Burr so far had been completely oblivious to the political situation. All around him hot-headed young men were arguing the cause of the colonies' freedom. While Alexander Hamilton was addressing crowds in

New York, stirring rebellion in the hearts of many, Burr enjoyed himself escorting the young ladies of Litchfield to picnics and parties. Summer seemed the wrong time to start work on so weighty a subject as law. He would wait until fall.

But fall came and went, and winter, too, without much studying on Burr's part. Then one fine April day a rider tore through Litchfield, spreading the news of the battles of Lexington and Concord.

This was action and suddenly Burr became conscious of the war. He had read history. He felt he knew all about sieges and battles. He felt he knew all about military leadership. Now was his chance to put his ideas to use. He threw aside his law books and started packing.

He wrote his friend Matthias Ogden, urging him to join up with him. When Ogden was slow to answer Burr rode to Elizabethtown to hurry him. By July, 1775, the two had made their way to Cambridge, proudly bearing a letter to General Washington from John Hancock, president of the Continental Congress, recommending "Mr. Ogden and Mr. Burr of the Jerseys."

The Commander in Chief had little time for letters

of recommendation. He was faced with an almost impossible task that summer in Boston. About him were gathered 17,000 untrained soldiers. There was no adequate way as yet to feed them, house them, clothe them, or arm them. The officers knew little more about warfare than the men.

Under these circumstances Washington had no time to welcome Aaron Burr to the Continental Army. Burr and Ogden wandered around, trying to find out when the fighting would start.

Then one day a rumor reached the camp. Benedict Arnold was leading an expedition from Newburyport, Massachusetts. The goal—to conquer Canada. This was what the boys had been waiting for—glorious adventure, sure to end in victory for the colonies.

Burr was ill with a fever but there was no time to lose. He clambered out of bed and walked all the way to Newburyport, a matter of some forty miles.

Uncle Timothy, hearing of his ward's intentions, dispatched a servant to stop him. The man caught up with Burr on a dusty road just outside Newburyport. He handed Aaron a stern letter from his uncle demanding that he return at once. Aaron read the letter, then looked at the servant.

"How do you expect to take me back if I refuse to go?" Aaron asked. "If you make one move to force me I'll have you hung up in ten minutes."

The servant looked blank. But Uncle Timothy knew his ward. He had prepared for this turn. The servant reached into another pocket and pulled out a second letter. This one begged Aaron not to go on the expedition and warned him of its hardships. Aaron laughed at it.

Uncle Timothy had expected that, too. This time the servant just handed him a bag of gold with his uncle's reluctant blessing.

· 5 ·

Bold
Failure

Excitement was great in Newburyport. All the volunteers had Burr's same impatience to get into battle. Bands played, women waved and wept. Eleven hundred men boarded the transports and sailed away to glory. The glory ended almost immediately when they hit a bad storm and most of the men—from Pennsylvania and Virginia and unaccustomed to the pitching of boats—wished they were dead.

Seven days later they reached Gardinierstown, at the mouth of the Kennebec River. Here they switched from the transports to 224 small boats, hastily built and overladen with men, provisions and heavy equipment.

The plan for this expedition was a bold one. Benedict Arnold was to march his men through the Maine wilderness to Quebec. At the same time, Generals Schuyler and Montgomery were to go from Fort Ticonderoga, which the Americans had captured, and strike at Montreal. The entire plan was based on surprise attack. Unfortunately, the surprise was for the Americans, not the British.

Arnold's timing was completely ruined by inaccurate maps of Maine. It took far longer to reach Quebec than he had planned.

The Kennebec River was treacherous. Boats overturned, or were tossed around so that they began to leak. Men had to get out in icy waters to try to repair them in order to save the supplies.

There were great distances where the boats had to be carried overland. As the weather grew colder, the food supply shorter, sickness flared through the forces.

They reached the Dead River on October 8th.

Arnold, pleased to have gotten so far, sent letters to Canada announcing his imminent arrival. The two Indians who carried the messages were captured. The British now had plenty of time to prepare.

If the first part of the trip had seemed perilous, it was nothing compared to the second part. The Dead River flooded and washed away all but a few of the boats. The men were soaked, their clothing ragged, their supplies gone. Aaron Burr and Matthias Ogden were in that brave advance guard. They poled boats, struggled in swampy bogs, waded in the freezing water, tried to help the sick, and ate whatever they could find—dog meat, soup made from shoes and what little game could be caught.

In desperation, Arnold sent men back to the rear guard to get reinforcements and provisions. The rear guard was of no help. It had deserted and returned home.

By the time they reached Quebec, only five hundred of the eleven hundred soldiers remained. The little band faced the fortress of Quebec with no heavy artillery, limited gun powder and meager rations. Arnold dispatched a message to Montgomery in Montreal, begging him to send help. Montgomery came himself, but he only had three hundred men to contribute to the assault.

Burr took an immediate liking to General Montgomery and the General was impressed by the bright young soldier. He had him transferred to his staff and promoted him to captain—at the age of nineteen.

At last he was to see action. Not being modest, young Burr had suggestions to make on how to attack Quebec. The city was walled, defended by two thousand British soldiers, and situated by nature so that it was perfectly protected. There was one place so high that it was almost impossible to scale. Burr suggested that the attack be made at this spot which the British would feel was safe and therefore would leave carelessly guarded.

It was a brave idea and might have worked. But Arnold and Montgomery chose the more conventional way. Each would attack from a different angle and meet—if all went well—in the heart of the city.

The plan meant that Montgomery and Burr were to take the lower town, where the business and shipping were situated. The British protected this with a blockhouse which could be reached only by entering a long, narrow path.

On a December night, under cover of a blinding snowstorm, Montgomery gave orders to attack. He and Burr and ten other hand-picked officers and men led the advance. They cut through the first barricade, crawled on in deep snow until they were almost on the blockhouse.

The English held their fire until the last minute, then let go with everything they had. Cannon and grapeshot swept the narrow pass. When the smoke cleared, only Burr was still standing. Montgomery lay dead in the snow. The others all were dead or badly wounded. Aaron tried to carry the gallant general back to the American lines, but he was too heavy for the slight young captain.

Burr returned to the waiting men and begged them to attack again. The men fled. He raced after them, urged, ordered, threatened them—but they would not enter the narrow pass. Burr's instinct had been correct. If he could have attacked again, he could have seized the blockhouse. After the first round of shot the British had taken to the hills. Burr had lost his chance to become a military hero.

Benedict Arnold's group fared little better. Arnold was wounded and another general captured. The Con-

Cannon and grapeshot swept the narrow pass.

tinental Army retired to count its losses. They were heavy, the men discouraged. Smallpox swept through the camp killing many. It was obvious no attack could continue, but the Americans held on until May. By then the British had brought up such quantities of reinforcements that all chance of a successful attack was gone.

Burr, knowing that no further war would be fought

in Quebec, was anxious to be off. His friend Ogden, who had returned to the fighting in New Jersey and had been made a colonel, wrote him of an opening on Washington's staff.

Burr told General Arnold he wanted to leave. The General wasn't too pleased but in a volunteer army there was little he could do. Then, too, he and Burr had not gotten on too well since he had rejected Burr's suggestion about scaling the heights of Quebec. The young captain did not take orders easily, Arnold had found. Let Washington have him!

Burr made his way back to New York in June. He was assigned to Washington's headquarters at Richmond Hill, the magnificent estate which was later to play a large part in Burr's life. But he was given paper work. What he longed for was battle. Again John Hancock appealed on his behalf and he was transferred to the staff of that old Connecticut warrior, General Israel Putnam.

Burr's start as a soldier had not been auspicious. But neither had Hamilton's. The same was true of the whole Continental Army. The beginning of the Revolution was all but disastrous!

· 6 ·

Chance
Meeting

General Howe had landed troops on Long Island and attacked New York. His well-trained, well-equipped army had little trouble advancing against the green "rebel" soldiers. The early British successes were overwhelming.

General Washington had no choice but to retreat. It was a dangerous maneuver across the river back to Manhattan Island. His men knew little about military tactics. It was pouring rain most of the time. There was great confusion.

Captain Hamilton and his company were part of this retreating army. He led his men well and kept them in order. Finally they reached a small fort which had been taken over by General Henry Knox. Knox, with more bravery than good military sense, had decided to defend the fort.

It was at this point that Aaron Burr, now a major, came upon them. He himself was cut off from General Putnam's army.

"Why haven't you retreated?" he asked the demoralized men.

General Knox replied that he and the men would make a stand.

"And die like dogs?" Burr shouted. "Follow me. If you die at least you die bravely and not as fools!"

Burr and Hamilton must have faced each other at some time during the harangue that followed—two keen, young, ambitious officers—Burr, twenty, dark and with piercing black eyes; Hamilton, twenty-one, fair, and ruddy-cheeked. It is possible that this is the first time that they met.

The honors went to Burr. The men rallied round

him, urging him to lead them. He did, even General Knox following, sullen and angry. Through back roads and over rough terrain Burr led the way until they were all safely behind the army's lines at Harlem Heights—including Alexander Hamilton. What was he thinking as he thanked Burr?

· 7 ·

Washington's
Right Hand

There were dark days ahead for the Continental Army. Washington's military tactics were brilliant, but brilliant in defeat rather than in victory. Every major battle had been lost, hundreds of men had deserted. The revolution itself was in danger.

Washington crossed the Delaware—you've seen the famous picture—and led his bedraggled men across New Jersey.

Lord Cornwallis, one of the British generals, almost caught up with them. He might have if it had not been for Hamilton and his battery. They were assigned to delay the British crossing of the Raritan River and did so with skillful artillery fire. Washington and his men were able to reach Princeton. He sent for Hamilton and congratulated him on his cool and clever bravery.

And he sent for him again not long after when winter camp had been set up at Morristown. Washington had long sought a competent aide, someone "who can think for me as well as execute orders."

It was an important post—important politically as well as from a military standpoint. The aide was to be, in effect, Washington's secretary. Hamilton had made a good record as a soldier. There were also many to testify to his political keenness.

Oddly enough, he did not want to take the post. He wanted instead the kind of glory won in battle. But Washington told him he wanted him and no one could refuse the Commander in Chief. So at twenty-one Hamilton became a lieutenant colonel—the eyes and ears, and sometimes the voice, through his pen, of the most important figure on the American scene.

The war dragged on. General Burgoyne—his troops called him "Gentleman Johnny"—pushed down from Canada. He was ordered by the King to join General Howe. Had he done so their combined forces might have won a quick victory. But Howe did not do his share. He was a lazy general and not too smart. He decided to take Philadelphia.

Washington tried to prevent this but lost the Battle of Brandywine. Howe and Burgoyne did not get together, but at the moment that seemed small comfort, for Washington had to retreat again.

Wars were different then. Armies did not fight in the winter. They waited out the ice and snow. The British spent the cold months at Philadelphia in comparative comfort. The unhappy Continental Army straggled on to Valley Forge in Pennsylvania and prepared to spend the winter there.

Then from the north came thrilling news. Burgoyne had started to join Howe as ordered. He had taken Fort Ticonderoga without trouble. It had seemed so easy that perhaps be became overconfident. Perhaps the rebels sensed this. At any rate they fought with more determination. And they were able to slow down the British advance.

Then at Saratoga something happened. The British were becoming weary. The Continentals pulled themselves together and took heart. They saw a chance to surround Burgoyne and his men. They closed in from every side. They fought with confidence and courage. The British were caught in a trap. Vainly they tried to force their way out. They couldn't. Finally, on October 17, 1777, badly defeated and with no hope of escape, Burgoyne surrendered.

This was something to make even the distressed Washington take heart. Now he saw a chance. If General Gates, whose army had won this battle of Saratoga, could send several divisions of men to join Washington's forces, the tide might be turned.

This wasn't so simple as it sounded. Gates was a vain, blustery soldier. He hadn't even bothered to let Washington know about his victory. He was reveling in his success. He would not be easy to deal with. Already there were those in Congress who were talking of Gates replacing Washington at the head of the army.

Washington delegated the delicate task of obtaining aid from General Gates to the charmer of his

Hamilton's battery delayed the British crossing.

staff—Hamilton. The young aide found Gates wallow-
ing in flattery. Messages of congratulations swamped
him. He listened to Hamilton. Immediately he was
suspicious. Did Washington mean to rob him of his
glory as well as his men?

Hamilton pleaded with all his persuasiveness for
three brigades. At first Gates would have none of it.
Let Washington win his own victories! Hamilton,
holding his hot temper, threw in every argument.

Gates finally yielded to the extent of one brigade
—General Patterson's. Hamilton spent the night
writing to Washington, telling him the situation. He
was, he said, afraid to argue further for fear of losing
the one brigade.

The next morning he went to inspect Patterson's
brigade. What he saw was a sadly depleted outfit—
barely six hundred men.

That was enough! Hamilton did not dare face
Gates for he knew his temper would explode. He
wrote him a letter so hot his pen almost burned the
paper. This time he didn't ask, he demanded help.

It was a gamble. He waited for the explosion. It
didn't come. Instead, General Gates reconsidered.
He would send not only Patterson's brigade but Gen-

eral Glover's, too. Hamilton did not wait for him to change his mind. He started back immediately.

On his way Hamilton stopped for a night at the home of General Philip Schuyler, near Albany. General Schuyler was a loyal supporter of Washington. His was a sympathetic ear for he had no liking for Gates who, through political maneuvers, had succeeded him as commander of the northern army.

The Schuylers were aristocrats, descendants of early Dutch patroons. This night in a soft bed in the great mansion of one of the richest men in the land must have been an experience for Hamilton, young soldier from a humble home, used now to the tough life of a soldier.

He would have liked to stay longer for he was tired and ill and needed rest. There was another reason, too. Her name was Elizabeth Schuyler—Betsey, her family called her. She was stunning, with dark, lively eyes that matched her black hair. And she was gay and warm. Alex needed gaiety and warmth.

But the next morning he pressed on. By the time he reached Valley Forge he was a sick man. What he faced there was even worse than illness. The story of that winter at Valley Forge is a dark chapter.

Washington's army, discouraged by defeat, suffered through bitter cold, with not enough clothing to cover them, not enough food to nourish them and little to which to look forward. They left blood on the snow when they walked in almost bare feet, and the suffering they were forced to undergo left a blot on the pages of our history.

Only one development of the winter brought hope. France came into the war on our side and against her old enemy, England. Eventually, Rochambeau and Lafayette were to arrive with troops and Admiral de Grasse with warships. But this was small cheer for the suffering troops at Valley Forge. Hamilton shared their hardships. But he had something to buoy him up—two keen black eyes that smiled at him over the miles.

· 8 ·

A Soldier
Who Couldn't Obey
Orders

As the war went on Burr's army career became a com-
bination of brilliance, bravery, and disobedience. The
same behavior which had made his mother say he
needed a "good governor" and which had driven his
poor Uncle Timothy nearly crazy, came out in his
attitude toward army orders. He simply felt he knew
better. Many times he was brighter than the officers
giving the orders. Many times his suggestions, had

they been accepted, might have changed the tide of the Revolution. But the fact remains that in the army you take orders from your superior officer—and Burr did not take orders easily.

He had been with General Putnam almost a year without a promotion—a fact that did not please him —when he received word from General Washington announcing his appointment as lieutenant colonel and his position as aide to Colonel William Malcolm, who commanded a regiment at Ramapo.

Command is perhaps too extravagant a word for Colonel Malcolm's duties. He was a merchant who, as was the custom with men of wealth, had equipped and raised a regiment. In return for this service, the regiment was named for him and he was commissioned a colonel and put in charge.

Malcolm had gathered round him as officers young sons of wealthy families. It was a tossup as to who knew less about military command—Malcolm or his officers. Things had gone from bad to worse. The two hundred and sixty men of the regiment were becoming unmanageable. Burr was sent to straighten things out.

Malcolm was more than willing to turn the entire

mess over to Burr. He immediately retired to a safe distance with his family. As he departed, he laid his hand on the young officer's capable shoulder.

"You shall have all the honor of fighting and disciplining the regiment," he said, "while I shall be its father."

The first thing Burr did was to draw on his own small income to pay the men. Then he discharged eleven of the incapable officers. In so doing he offended one who evidently resented losing his handsome uniform, and narrowly missed his first duel.

Burr set up drills and inspections and saw that his disgruntled soldiers were made to toe the mark. Within two months the Malcolms were a first-class regiment and Aaron Burr was the idol of his men.

In September, 1777, news was received that the King's Royal Governor had gathered together two thousand men and was advancing toward Orange County, stealing and plundering on the way. Burr immediately set forth with the Malcolms to oppose them. He had no sooner begun to march than a messenger galloped up with orders from General Putnam to retire with the public stores into the mountains. The enemy force, he felt, was too great to meet.

Twenty-one-year-old Burr looked squarely at the messenger.

"I cannot run away from an enemy I haven't seen. Please tell General Putnam I will be answerable for the public stores and for my men," he announced firmly.

He spurred his horse to the front of the line and ordered the advance to continue. There was nothing for the messenger to do but return to General Putnam.

When Burr and his men reached Paramus, they found the town in great confusion, believing an attack would begin at any moment. Burr left the regiment to guard the town and with thirty of his own men and some guides he moved forward to reconnoiter the enemy.

He found them—at least the outposts—some three miles from Hackensack. Leaving his men to rest, he went alone to spy out the size of the British force. He returned, awakened his small group, and led a night assault. All of the British outpost were killed or taken prisoner. Burr had not lost a man.

He sent an express rider to Paramus to bring up the regiment and rally the countryside. The British, however, did not wait to see more of Burr. By morning they had fled, leaving their cannon and the loot

Leaving his men, Burr spied on the British force.

they had stolen. Burr was all for pursuing them, but this time General Putnam sent a command which could not be disobeyed. Burr was to return at once and join the main body of the Continental Army in Pennsylvania. Instead of glory, Burr marched off for a winter at Valley Forge.

By now Burr's success in pulling together a hopeless regiment and making it one of the best had reached headquarters. Although Washington turned down a plan submitted by Burr for taking Staten Island, he did send him on a very ticklish mission.

A body of militia guarded an important pass about eight miles from camp. The discipline was bad; in fact, the men were close to mutiny. Burr was sent to put them back in shape—if possible.

He took command. In his usual thorough way he drilled them, trained them, started a strict system of policing, and paid unexpected visits to check up on them. The men resented this little officer who looked younger than his years. He issued orders and he expected them to be obeyed. They decided to murder him.

Burr, who all his life seemed to know what was going on before it happened, found out about the plot. Secretly he had all the cartridges removed from the muskets while the men slept. Then—in the middle of the night—he paraded the regiment for inspection. Saber in hand he marched along the ranks of angry men.

Suddenly the ringleader leaped out of line, leveled his musket, and shouted:

"Now is the time, my boys!"

With a flash the Colonel's sword ripped through the soldier's arm.

"Take your place in line, sir," Burr ordered the man.

No one moved except the wounded soldier, who humbly obeyed.

The mutiny was over, the regiment in shape again, but Burr was not thanked. The soldier lost his arm and instead of a citation, the Colonel narrowly missed being court-martialed.

As winter passed to spring the war was resumed. General Clinton decided to evacuate Philadelphia and retire to New York. Washington ordered his army to pursue the enemy. General Lee was to lead the advance guard with orders to attack as soon as he spotted the British.

For some reason he got as far as Monmouth and then retreated, telling his young assistant, the Marquis de Lafayette, who was protesting:

"Sir, you do not know British soldiers. We cannot stand against them."

His retreat not only threw away all chance of success but seriously threatened the left flank of the American army.

The Colonel's sword ripped through the soldier's arm.

Washington, seeing what Lee had done, galloped up in a fury, blustered until the leaves shook on the trees. He took command himself and tried to save the situation from disaster. He threw out a battle line to check the British. The formation—hastily drawn— was as brilliant as any tactician could wish. Its left and right flanks rested on natural obstructions. Its center—like a sling shot—took its strength from each end.

Burr was in command of three regiments, including his own Malcolms; his orders were merely to hold his flank position while the center of the line did the fighting. Two young officers—Lafayette and Hamilton —were in that center, leading charges and gathering glory. For Burr it was impossible to stand by and watch.

Suddenly he saw his chance. A small British detachment was breaking out of the woods across the swamp. A swift move would cut them off from support. He had no orders to attack, but delay might lose this chance. The headstrong Burr signaled his men.

Washington spotted this disobedience and immediately sent his aide, Lieutenant Colonel Francis Barber, to halt the attack. A weakening of that flank could turn his entire plan of battle into a disaster.

The regiments were halfway through the swamp when a hidden battery opened up and ripped them to pieces. Barber gave the Commander in Chief's orders to Burr. Now that the damage was done, Burr's only hope was to unite his three regiments on the other side of the swamp. Every Malcolm who fell broke his heart. He wanted to save as many as possible. This he explained to Barber. The Commander's orders were repeated and this time Burr obeyed.

He had led his men into a trap. He would bring them out. Lashing his horse into the thickest of the volley, he urged his men, entreated them, encouraged them. A cannon ball hit his horse. Burr continued on foot.

He led his Malcolms back, but only a third of them reached safety. That night he nursed the wounded, cheered the discouraged, and looked for the dead.

Morning came. The British had continued their retreat under darkness. Burr, exhausted and sick, threw himself down to sleep.

This was his last battle. His health was bad, and though he stayed in the army for a short time doing intelligence work, he was never again to lead the Malcolms.

Perhaps it was just as well. General Washington, while admitting his ability, was tired of young Burr's stubborn disregard for orders.

· 9 ·

The Colonel
Takes a Wife

While Burr was disobeying orders at the Battle of
Monmouth, Hamilton was obeying them. He con-
tributed his share to the victory. It was an important
victory, too, even though the British did manage to
get most of their men to New York, where they settled down for another winter's lull.

There was no Valley Forge for the Continental
Army this time. Washington established winter quar-

ters at Morristown, New Jersey. Food was plentiful; the men had better and warmer clothing; quarters were almost luxurious by comparison, and the winter was a mild one.

Hamilton had his duties—missions of various kinds, some of them simple and some dangerous. But he had time, too, to take a clear look at the political situation. What he saw was lack of unity, petty bickering in Congress, looming financial difficulties and the great need of central power and authority among the loosely bound colonies.

It was a time of gaiety, too. There was a new feeling of confidence in the air. The married officers were joined by their wives. Martha Washington came up from Virginia to join the General. And there were many charming young ladies near by to make life a little merrier for the unmarried officers. It all developed into something of a social season.

Hamilton found plenty of time to join in this round of entertainment. And to his surprise at a ball one evening he found himself looking into the dark eyes of Betsey Schuyler again. She was visiting her aunt, Mrs. John Cochran, wife of the Surgeon General, in Morristown.

Only a year before Hamilton had written to his old friend, John Laurens, in South Carolina:

"Do I want a wife? No. I have plagues enough without desiring to add to the number that greatest of all."

If he had really meant that statement he soon changed his mind. There were sleigh rides and formal dinners and gay dances and Betsey was his companion at all. He wrote a friend that Betsey, or Eliza, as he sometimes liked to call her, "had found out the secret of interesting me in everything that concerns her." He lost his head to the point that one night when returning to quarters after leaving her at the Cochran home, he was challenged by a sentry and couldn't remember the password.

Missions on which he was sent now by General Washington were just an interruption to his courtship.

In September, 1780, he and General Washington went to Hartford to confer with the French, hoping to plan with them an attack on New York. On their way back they stopped off at West Point, the key fortress between New England and the other colonies. It was then commanded by General Benedict Arnold.

When they reached the fort, General Arnold was

not there. He had left after receiving a letter delivered by a messenger, even though he knew the Commander in Chief was coming. Hamilton talked to Mrs. Arnold and found her in a highly nervous state. He sensed something was wrong.

Before the day was out another messenger with a report for General Washington arrived. It was news that a man giving the name of John Anderson had been arrested. He had been identified as a British officer, Major John André. In his stocking was concealed valuable information and a plan of the fort at West Point which would have made its capture easy. To get through the lines he had used a pass signed by General Benedict Arnold!

General Washington went into action. Arnold's rooms were searched and they revealed evidence that, embittered by the fact that many officers had been promoted over him, he had sold out to the British.

Arnold had several hours' start and it was reported his barge had been seen going downriver. Hamilton and a few other officers were dispatched on horseback to head him off, but he reached a British warship, the *Vulture,* in the Hudson River and escaped.

It was a black chapter in American history.

Two months later, Hamilton was off on another mission, but one of which Betsey approved, for it was for his marriage to her. It took place in Albany on December 14, 1780, with a great reception afterward at the Schuyler mansion. Betsey went back with him to army headquarters where she was made welcome by no less a matron than Martha Washington.

The war limped on. It was a slow business, this fight for independence. Hamilton was restless. Perhaps he did not know what he wanted. There were times when he sought more action in the field. He had become a close friend of the Marquis de Lafayette, who wanted to attack New York. Hamilton was to command troops in the venture. But evidently the plan was vetoed.

There were other times when his ambitions seemed to be political. Mistakes had been made. The country's credit was going to pieces. The people, loaded with war burdens, were becoming afraid of what this liberty for which they fought might mean. Hamilton was worried, too. He set to work on plans for the new nation, but without much help. He was frustrated and restless, discontented and impatient. Something was bound to happen.

"You have kept me waiting these ten minutes."

In February, 1781, it did. It was at headquarters in New Windsor. Hamilton was taking a letter to another officer. He passed General Washington on the stairs.

"I wish to speak to you," said the General.

"I will wait upon you immediately, sir," said Hamilton.

He went downstairs, delivered the letter, and was on his way back when he was detained for a moment or two by the Marquis de Lafayette. When he reached the bend of the stairs, General Washington was waiting for him, his face red below his white wig.

"Colonel Hamilton," he said testily, "you have kept me waiting these ten minutes. I must tell you, sir, you treat me with disrespect!"

Hamilton drew himself up.

"I am not conscious of it, sir," he said coldly, "but since you have thought it necessary to tell me so, we part."

They did—each striding off in anger.

· 10 ·

Victory!

Within an hour Washington's hot temper had cooled. He sent an aide to Hamilton urging that they both reconsider what had happened.

Hamilton replied that he had made his decision and would stand by it. From his determination it seems clear that he had planned to resign at the first opportunity and merely used the incident on the stairs as an excuse. He had long disliked his duties as aide.

Now that he was free he was still torn between the problems confronting the nation and the urge for military action. After a few months of inactivity he decided upon the latter. He wrote General Washington asking for command of a regiment.

Washington was in a difficult spot. He could not very well promote Hamilton over the heads of officers who had fought courageously in the field. Still he knew that if he did not give Hamilton a regiment the young officer would think he was refusing from spite. But his answer was no.

Hamilton turned his restless mind to the shaky financial condition of the government. His father-in-law urged him to go into Congress. But the war was still to be won and Hamilton wanted action in the field. Again, he asked for a command. Again, he was turned down. This time he wrote General Washington an angry letter telling him he was through with the war. Washington refused to let him resign.

Just as he had given up all hope, Hamilton's wish came true. Washington was planning an all-out attack on New York. He needed officers—able officers.

On July 31, 1781, he assigned Lieutenant Colonel Hamilton to command a battalion. At last Hamilton was happy.

Then, suddenly, plans were changed. The British were pouring reinforcements into New York. It would be a difficult task to dislodge them and would cost many men.

Washington now saw a new possibility. Part of the war had turned south. There were many loyalists there. Hoping for help from them, General Cornwallis had marched on Virginia. Lafayette was trying to stop him, but had too few soldiers. But he and Washington saw a chance to lead Cornwallis into a trap.

With utmost secrecy and still pretending to plan an attack on New York, Washington moved his army swiftly south by forced marches. Rochambeau quietly dispatched the French fleet, under Admiral de Grasse, in the same direction. Lafayette, falling back, lured Cornwallis and his army out on the peninsula of which Yorktown was the tip.

The French attacked the British fleet off Virginia and in a five-day battle scored a brilliant victory and sent it limping off to the North. French troops were

"We have it!" he shouted to his major.

landed on the peninsula. Washington's army arrived. Cornwallis did not know it but he was hemmed in.

Cornwallis had built two redoubts at Yorktown from which he could put any frontal attack under cross fire. Washington prepared to storm these. The French, under Baron de Viomenil, were in position to attack one. Hamilton was sure his battalion would be assigned to storm the other.

He waited for the orders. They came. The other redoubt was to be attacked by men under Lieutenant Colonel Barber!

Hamilton ran to Lafayette in a rage. The French general explained the order had come from Washington himself. Sure that the General had taken a personal revenge, Hamilton wrote him a scorching note. He was certain it would do no good but he felt he must be heard.

Then from Washington's headquarters came a new order. Lieutenant Colonel Hamilton's battalion would move against the left redoubt!

Hamilton read the order.

"We have it! We have it!" he shouted to his major.

At six o'clock on the evening of October 17th, cannon shot rang out signaling the attack. Lieutenant Colonel Hamilton was not content just to give the orders that sent his men forward. He had waited too long for this moment. He leaped from a parapet and led them himself.

The British did not surrender easily. It was close bayonet fighting. But they had their backs to the wall. The rebel charge was fierce. The redoubt was taken. The French charged, too, and were victorious.

Cornwallis now had no chance to escape. Two days later—on October 19th—he surrendered.

This was to prove the last battle of the war. The long struggle in the field was over. Independence had been won. However, George III was stubborn. Even in the face of defeat he didn't want to give up, but his people did not care to carry on the fight for colonies across a wide ocean.

There was no telegraph, no telephone. News had to be sent by messenger. It was five days later that the report of the victory at Yorktown reached Congress in Philadelphia.

When the messenger brought the news of this capitulation, Elias Boudinot later reported that "it was necessary to furnish him with hard money for his expenses. There was not a sufficiency in the Treasury to do it, and the members of Congress, of which I was one, each paid a dollar to accomplish it."

It was to this problem—a victorious but bankrupt new nation—that Alexander Hamilton was soon to turn his attention.

· 11 ·

Rivals—
and Friends

The peace treaty was not signed until 1783, but there
was no more fighting.

Burr, after his resignation, had attempted to regain
his health. It was a slow fight because he was worn
and tired. And he was torn by another problem, concern over which probably prolonged his period of re-
cuperation.

In 1777, while stationed in New Jersey, he had met

Mrs. Theodosia Prevost who lived with her five children in Paramus. She was not beautiful, but she was
brilliant and had great charm. She and Burr had
many interests in common—books, art and the whole
realm of ideas. The young major fell in love with her.

However, instead of joy this brought deep concern.
She was married to another. That was trouble enough.
But it was more than that. Her husband was a British
officer, Lieutenant Colonel Jacques Marc Prevost, on
duty in the West Indies; and she was, technically, an
enemy.

By birth Mrs. Prevost was an American, her mother
the daughter of one of the early settlers of Virginia,
her father an honored lawyer of New Jersey. But two
of her sons were serving in the British navy. She was
eyed with suspicion by her neighbors but liked by
many of the Continental officers including General
Washington.

This situation could not but weigh heavily on
Burr's mind. He retired to New Haven when he left
his army duties and did his best to recover his health.
But his life was aimless and he had no interest. He
was restless. His funds were running short.

Then suddenly came news of the death of Lieu-

tenant Colonel Prevost in the West Indies. The effect
on Burr was electric. All his old energy and ambition
returned. He was ready to start life anew. He returned
eagerly again to his interest in the law.

The legal profession offered unusual opportunities
in the new nation which was being formed. Almost all
the great lawyers of the time were Tories. Their loyalty was to British law. So there was a revolution in
the legal profession, too. There were demands that
all who would not take the new oath of loyalty be
disqualified from practice.

This became a law in October, 1781. Burr was eager
to qualify at once. He had studied for almost a year,
but three years were required. Burr was a born politician. By clever maneuvering, he managed to clear
the way and to pass the examination. In April, 1782,
he was admitted to practice. Old Dr. Bellamy, his
erstwhile teacher, congratulated him and remarked
dryly:

"With your few months of study, I wonder you
know enough to keep the law, let alone going about
its practice!"

But Judge Smith, with whom Burr had studied law,
knew his pupil better than Dr. Bellamy.

"Mark my words," he told a fellow member of the bar, "should you be someday pitted against him, you will find him possessed of this sinister peculiarity: If he's right, you won't defeat him; if he's wrong, exercise your utmost care, or he will defeat you."

Three months later, having launched on a successful career in Albany with an overabundance of clients, Aaron Burr married Theodosia Prevost.

Hamilton, by a curious parallel of paths that was to follow them always, had turned to the law, too. In the fall of 1781, all fighting having come to a stop, he went to Albany to join his wife. And in January of 1782, a son was born to them whom they named Philip, the first of eight children.

General Schuyler was eager for his son-in-law to become a member of Congress, to get right into the work of building the foundation of the new nation. But now that he was a father, Hamilton felt the need of a profession, and he did not want to accept financial assistance from his generous father-in-law. He had quietly been reading Blackstone, the great legal expert, for months. Now he went at his studies earnestly. Robert Troup, his old college mate, moved into the Hamilton home and the two of them worked together far into every night. By the following autumn, Hamilton passed his examinations and was ready to practice.

The Burrs also lived in Albany. There on June 21, 1783, a girl was born to them. They named her Theodosia after her mother. A second daughter was born later, but lived only a few years. Theodosia lived to be her father's great joy, a darling girl, a brilliant woman, almost a legend before her tragic end.

Albany was a happy place for these two young families, but New York held greater prospects for ambitious lawyers.

The city was growing and thriving. Its harbor was the best on the Atlantic coast. New York had the future of a metropolis. It would become the capital of peacetime enterprise.

Anticipating that moment, Burr borrowed money and rented a house on Wall Street, next door but one to City Hall.

Hamilton, too, saw that his future was in the city. Here there were unlimited possibilities for social, economic and political adventure. The one profession that opened on all three was the law. Hamilton took his law degree and moved his little family to 57 Wall Street—only a short distance from Burr. They were friendly neighbors now, and no one could foresee the bitter rivalry which lay ahead.

· 12 ·

Little Young
New York

The New York these young men found was quite different in size from what it is today. The population was not quite 30,000. Of houses, there were about 3,000, mostly built of brick with tiled roofs.

Streets were narrow and crooked. Some were paved, but most were dirt—dusty in summer, muddy in winter. There were few sidewalks. Refuse was dumped in the middle of the streets where time, sun, rain and the neighbors' pigs were supposed to do the work of the street-cleaning department.

Goats, pigs and dogs ran freely, thereby adding to the traffic problem which was already great. The city fathers were struggling with the problem then as now. They enacted a law requiring that "persons meeting on the highway, those going out of the city north-ward are to make room for those coming southward under penalty of 40 shillings fine for failure to do so."

It was undoubtedly a kindness to let carriages coming into the city have the right of way. A traveler coming from Boston might have spent eight days sitting upright in a rocking coach. Roads were terrible and the lack of springs made every bump an insult to the spine. At night the stages stopped at a tavern, and from ten in the evening until two in the morning the weary passengers were allowed to rest. Then the coach horn awakened them rudely to another day of tossing and bouncing. It was a welcome relief when the coach was bogged down, or the hill too steep for the horses, and the travelers were allowed to get out and walk or, if need be, help push.

Fares were about four cents a mile. A coach ride to Boston was a little more expensive than a train ride nowadays.

The Hamiltons and the Burrs probably chose another form of transportation from Albany—a sailing sloop. The Hudson River—even in rough weather—provided much more comfort than the roads. Of course, you could not count on time. With luck you might make it in two days. Without luck—which meant against wind and tide—it might take you nine.

Betsey's first morning in New York must have been a surprise to her after the quiet of Albany. From dawn on, business took place noisily outside every house.

The milk maid carried her buckets suspended from a yoke and cried, "Milk ho! Milk come!" as she walked by. In warm weather, it was better to buy early or your milk would sour.

Next came chimney sweeps, important in that day when a dirty flu could cause a bad fire and lose you your house. As the cry, "Sweep ho! Sweep ho!" faded down the street, the water vendor would appear. New York had no water supply in those days. Citizens had to depend on ponds and wells, most of which were so contaminated that even the horses refused to drink the water from them. So for your drinking water, you bought by the gallon from the lucky owner of the Tea-Water Well—the only decent water in the city.

More tradesmen followed—knife grinders, ragmen, lamp menders, and wood sellers, and they all raised their voices. If you bought wood, the seller set up his saw in front of your house and added to the traffic jam while he cut your order.

Pigs squealing, dogs barking, church bells ringing, all added to the general din. It was necessary to stretch a chain across the street in front of the Merchants Exchange where the court met so that the judges could hear themselves think.

A housewife had her hands full. The young Burrs and Hamiltons probably had a servant or two, but even so, the running of the house fell largely on the mistresses' shoulders.

Betsey must have started out to market those first days curious and eager to see what the big city had to offer. Old Swago Market, Exchange Market, Bear Market and Fly Market (the oldest, but with the oddest name) all had much to offer. White bread was six cents a pound, rye bread three cents cheaper. Beei was six and a half cents a pound; ham, seven cents. Butter also cost seven cents and in summer you rushed home to put it in your cool cellar.

There were plenty of apples, pears and peaches, but bananas, oranges and pineapples were luxuries to be bought only by the rich at Peter Deschant's or Cato Railmore's on Broadway.

On her way home Betsey could not window-shop, for few shops had any windows in which to show their wares. She would, however, pass by many where wine and tobacco, tea and coffee, molasses and sugar could all be bought.

In most cases, the front room of the lower floor of your home served as your office. Therefore, when Betsey returned from market, she caught a glimpse of her husband bent over his law books.

Theodosia Burr, being older and more experienced, would not be so impressed with New York. She was never the housewife and hostess that Betsey Hamilton grew to be. Her interests were in books and music, and with her husband she shared the task of educating their children.

Her two sons were studying law and helping their stepfather in his office. Little Theo was the center of the household. Aaron Burr had decided at her birth that she should grow up to be the living proof of his theory that women were as bright as men—a startling viewpoint in 1780! From babyhood on, he laid down a schedule of learning which was to make her the best-educated woman in the country. Even when Burr was out of town on a law case, which happened frequently, he would write to know of Theo's progress, and Mrs. Burr must answer in full.

Her problem was not in writing the answer, but in getting it delivered to her Aaron as soon as possible. Mails arrived and left the city three times a week. The post office was in the postmaster's house, however inconveniently that might be situated for the citizens. Rates were high—ten cents for one sheet to Philadelphia, thirty-three cents to Savannah. And, of course, there was no guarantee the letter would ever reach its destination.

The most satisfactory way was to find someone journeying in the right direction and then beg him to carry the letter to your loved one. The Burrs seemed to have depended on this system, as so many notes begin, "Your letter by Mr. Bayard was brought to me on Saturday. . . ."

Business took place noisily outside every house. Trade

men, pedestrians and carriages thronged the streets.

When Aaron Burr was in town he was a frequent user of the New York Society Library. Both his name and Hamilton's appeared on their records, but Burr's more often. He was an avid reader.

Both men must have subscribed to the *Daily Advertiser* or the *Daily Gazette*. These newspapers cost six dollars a year if brought to your home, or four cents a copy if you called for them at the printers. News from abroad was somewhat old, an October copy carrying a letter from London dated July, but the advertisements and the public notices were up to date.

The year 1783 found Hamilton and Burr the two most sought-after lawyers in New York. Burr's fee was somewhat higher than Hamilton's, but each had quickly taken his place at the top of their profession.

Hamilton was careful and painstaking. He worked out every detail of a case. He was an orator. His style was clear and shining, his choice of words keen and cutting.

Burr was quick of mind. He went at once to the essentials of an argument and lost no time on elaborate building of a case. His style was simple and conversational, not oratorical. It is said that he never lost a case that he personally handled.

The two met frequently as opponents in the courts. There was at least one time when they worked side by side on a case—the first real murder mystery in the history of New York. They were joint counsel for the defense.

The body of Elma Sands, a young girl, had been found in a well in Lespenard's Meadow, a lonely spot then, but now part of New York's teaming East Side.

A young man named Levi Weeks, who rented a room in the home of the young lady's aunt and uncle with whom she lived, was arrested. The evidence was circumstantial and largely supplied by Richard Croucher, another lodger. Burr and Hamilton joined in defending the accused.

There is a story that, at the trial, Croucher, the chief witness, was being cross-examined by Burr. The lawyer's sharp and searching questions led the witness into deeper and deeper confusion. Then suddenly, according to the story, Burr picked up a candlestick from the counsel table and held it close to Croucher's face.

"Gentlemen of the jury," he shouted, "behold the murderer."

Croucher, it is said, jumped to his feet and ran shrieking from the courtroom. The verdict in the case was "not guilty."

The story is legendary. There are no court records to verify it. But at least Burr and Hamilton, working together, won an acquittal for their client. What might have happened if they had continued to work together not only in the courts but in the field of politics as well?

· 13 ·

From Sword
to Pen

Politics was to be the field of battle in which Alexander Hamilton and Aaron Burr fought, literally, to the death.

But at this dawning day of the new nation the lines of battle were not drawn. This was due to the fact that Burr took very little interest in the laying of the foundation of our government. It was when he discovered that politics could be a source of power that he became interested. He was to become a politician rather than a statesman—one who used politics rather than letting political developments use him to build a strong and free and lasting government.

Nothing would have kept Hamilton out of the political surge. All through his service in the army, particularly when he was General Washington's aide, he watched the problems the Revolution faced and looked ahead to see what could be done to solve them and to chart a course for the government.

These were genuine problems, too. The thirteen colonies were being ruled by a Continental Congress. There was no strong executive. The Congress decided everything. All laws had to be passed by nine of the thirteen colonies. The Congress operated under Articles of Federation adopted in 1777 to which some of the colonies had been opposed and even now did not support wholeheartedly. All this did not make for unity.

The nation was deeply in debt. Soldiers were demanding back pay. There were the nations which had lent us money to be paid. There was little "hard money" and the paper money was practically valueless. You've heard the expression, "Not worth a continental." It meant not worth a continental paperback.

And to make matters worse, Congress couldn't raise money by taxation. All it could do was ask the states for money. That didn't mean it would get any. During the Revolution it asked the states for ten million dollars and got less than a fourth of it.

Hamilton knew these things. Already his keen young mind was working on the financial problems. He had ideas. But they would not work without a real government to back them up.

Some way had to be found to make all the states realize they had to be bound together more effectively. When, at a meeting of representatives of Virginia and Maryland on a minor matter which concerned only the two states, Virginia proposed a convention to include all the states for a discussion of trade problems, Hamilton was quick to see the value of the suggestion.

The convention was called. It met at Annapolis, Maryland, but most states were suspicious of the move. Only five sent delegates. Hamilton was present as a New York representative. Undaunted at the small attendance, he saw to it that the group passed a resolution urging a fully attended convention to discuss all the problems of the country, not just a few.

A short but fiery "rebellion" in Massachusetts, led by Daniel Shays, and the general unrest which followed, worked in Hamilton's favor. Congress finally took the recommendation seriously, and officially scheduled such a convention to be held in Philadelphia May 25, 1787.

All the colonies but little Rhode Island were represented when the Constitutional Convention, with fifty-five delegates, was called to order by George Washington. It was to make history, but during the many days that it met there seemed little indication of that. There were many times when it seemed almost certain to break up with no accomplishment. There was disagreement, quarreling, jealousy—oratory and just plain shouting. The little states were afraid that in any union they would be dominated by the big states. There were those who did not want the states to give up too many rights to a central government. The landed gentry feared the industrial and commercial group. Both were distrusted by everyone who did not belong to these classes.

There were even those who wanted a monarchy

with a king—a nice king, of course, and not one like
George III.

Day after day things went on seemingly without
hope. The finest minds of the nation could not get
together. Washington, Madison, Randolph, Franklin,
Morris, and Pinckney argued pro and con. Hamilton
poured forth all his theories of government in a brilliant speech but it fell on ears that were not all sympathetic. The bickering went on and on. It became
evident that whatever came out of the convention
would be compromise and Hamilton could not stand
compromise. He left the convention for a time but
could not stay away and came back to help hammer
the final document into shape.

Finally, on September 17, there emerged the
Constitution of the United States. We know it now
as probably the greatest government document of all
time, but it did not seem so then. It was a collec-
tion of divided opinions sewn together with compromise.

If adopted, it gave every promise of solving the
problems of the new nation. It divided government
into three branches—the legislative, to make the laws;

the judicial, to see that the laws were just; the executive, to enforce the laws.

It set up a Congress of two houses whose members voted as individuals, and not by states. And the members of these two houses of Congress had the power to tax. This was taxation *with* representation. The states retained many of their rights, but the federal government dominated the states in some matters. And the Constitution could be changed if the people wanted it changed.

Now that we know, through years of experience, what a great document it is, we find it difficult to believe that there was opposition to it then. But there was in many places—even high places. The battle was not over. The Constitution still had to be approved or ratified by the states.

In New York there was a strong faction against it. Even Hamilton found the document lacking in some ways, but he was broadminded enough to see that its unifying effect would be for the great good of the country. He threw himself whole-heartedly into the fight for ratification.

Governor Clinton of New York, a champion of states' rights, opposed it bitterly. Hamilton, knowing this, used every free moment to plead for the document. He had to return to his law practice—Betsey and the children couldn't live on ideals—but wherever he went, in taverns and courthouses and homes, he spoke ardently about the Constitution. He answered arguments, explained away objections. He pleaded and persuaded.

Then one day on his way home from Fishkill, all his ideas came into focus. Sitting in the cabin of a small sloop he forgot the beautiful scenery of the Hudson River. His pen traveled over paper at lightning speed. By the time he reached New York one of the greatest political treatises ever written had been finished.

This was the first of a series of eighty-five brilliant letters—known as the Federalist Papers—which contained every plea for the Constitution and for a central government. Hamilton wrote fifty-one of these; the others were the work of Madison and Jay, who joined him in the task. The Federalist Papers appeared not only in New York newspapers but elsewhere in the new nation. They had a tremendous effect on the people.

However, the voting was not to be done by the

On the sloop, Hamilton wrote the first Federalist paper.

people themselves. The battle had to be won in the individual state Constitutional Conventions.

Nine states were needed to make the Constitution legal. Slowly, one by one, states began to ratify. Delaware was the first, then Pennsylvania, then Georgia, New Jersey, Connecticut, Massachusetts, Maryland. It was getting closer. South Carolina fell into line, making eight. One more state was needed!

Hamilton was hopeful that New York would be the ninth—the deciding state. But now a new fear arose in him. The delegates to the New York Constitutional Convention were elected—Clinton won forty-six, Hamilton nineteen. What if New York did not ratify at all—was left out of the new union?

Virginia and New Hampshire were on the eve of casting their convention votes. Hamilton wrote to James Madison in Virginia:

"It will be of vast importance that an exact communication should be kept up between us. The moment *any decisive* question is taken, if favorable, I request you to dispatch an express to me, with pointed orders to make all possible diligence, by changing horses, etc. All expense shall be thankfully and liberally paid."

He sent much the same message to John Sullivan of New Hampshire, stressing the need for haste. Any favorable news might help him influence the delegates. This was his great hope.

The convention was held in the village of Poughkeepsie on June 17, 1788. Hamilton knew that if a vote was taken immediately he would lose. His only chance was to delay—to outtalk his opposition. From the moment the convention began he was on his feet arguing, imploring, explaining. Some of his speeches lasted two days. He repeated the same things over and over, fighting for time. It was the first filibuster!

Throughout the long days Hamilton had been listening for the sound of hoofbeats. On June 21st, after talking almost incessantly for four days, he heard what he had been waiting to hear. The express rider galloped up, lashing the final horse in the long breakneck relay from New Hampshire. The weary messenger thrust an envelope into Hamilton's hands.

Hamilton ripped it open. New Hampshire had ratified the Constitution—the ninth state! The United States was a nation!

But New York was not a part of that nation and Hamilton was determined that it should be. He rushed

to the floor of the convention and made the announcement. The Federalists cheered—but their joy was short.
The opposition was silent—only slightly impressed.
Hamilton fought on. Virginia was still to be heard
from, and Virginia was the most important state of
the new nation.

It was on June 25th that a second messenger came
thundering through the dusty streets of Poughkeepsie.
This time it was the long-awaited news from Madison
—Virginia had ratified. Now the tide seemed to be
turning. It was Governor Clinton's turn to fight. For
three weeks he sought in every way to defeat New
York's ratification. But Hamilton fought just as stub-
bornly.

It was July 25th before the motion was put to the
delegates. By this time it seemed sure that Clinton
had rallied his forces, that New York would remain
outside the union.

Then something almost miraculous took place before the eyes of the exhausted delegates. Melancton
Smith, Clinton's right-hand man who had been the
chief opponent of Hamilton in the speech-making,
rose. In a few startling sentences he announced
gravely that he had been convinced by Hamilton. He

cast his vote for the Constitution. Others followed now, and when the roll call was over ratification had won —by three votes.

The new union had a constitution and New York was in the union, thanks largely to Alexander Hamilton.

· 14 ·

The First
President

There was no question as to who should lead the new
nation. On April 30, 1789, George Washington stood
on the balcony of Federal Hall in Wall Street and
took the oath of office as the first President.

Betsey and the children watched from their house
across the way. They were fortunate to have such a
fine view of the proceedings for the streets were

jammed with people eager for a glimpse of America's hero.

The ceremony was a simple one. Washington, dressed in a rich brown coat and white linen, his powdered hair tied back, looked tall and stately as he stood with his hand on the Bible. The humility with which he added "So help me God" and kissed the Book made tears come to Betsey's eyes. The crowd was silent for one moment, overwhelmed by the occasion. Then it burst into wild cheering.

Betsey left the house and pushed her way through the crowd to join her husband. Together they went to St. Paul's Chapel for the service that followed.

For Betsey, this day marked a complete change in her home life. A wonderful wife and mother, she now had to become a ready hostess. Her husband had been made the nation's first Secretary of the Treasury and chose to entertain frequently.

Hamilton's manner was never more persuasive than at the dinner table. By candlelight he was his most handsome and charming self. Whenever a cause was to be sold, a bill to be passed, the Hamiltons would entertain. Betsey's budget was upset many a time. It wasn't easy to manage a large family on $3,000 a

year, Hamilton's salary. Especially as her husband
was too busy with the nation's financial problems to
attend to his own. Although he could account for every
penny in the United States Treasury, he never knew
how much money he had or how much he owed. Generous to a fault, his home was always a refuge for
any friend in need. Baron von Steuben lived with the
Hamiltons for years until he was finally given a government pension for his valiant services during the
Revolution. Later, Lafayette's young son was a permanent guest. Somehow Betsey stretched their little
income so capably that one admirer said to Hamilton:

"She has as much merit as your treasurer as you
have as treasurer of the wealth of the United States."

Among the frequent guests at the Hamilton house
were the Burrs. Betsey and Theodosia were friends
and young Angelica Hamilton and little Theo were
very close.

The Burrs had moved several times since their first
home on Queen Street. Each house was more elaborate than the last, but Aaron Burr would not be happy
until he could buy Richmond Hill—the home he had
seen as a young officer during the war. At the moment it was occupied by Vice President John Adams.

The Hamiltons had a front-window view of the inauguration.

Situated on a wooded height between meadows and brook and overlooking the Hudson River, it was a noble house. Inside there were magnificent high-ceil-inged rooms and mahogany staircases; outside a great portico of Ionic columns, surrounded by lawn and garden. No wonder Burr wished to own it.

For the time being, however, the Burrs lived in a pretty house on Nassau Street. From here they watched New York grow during that inaugural year. Being the seat of the new government, the city was crowded with congressmen, officials and visitors from abroad. Theodosia Burr was not well and did not attend many of the parties and balls and "at homes" that winter, but she heard about them from Betsey Hamilton.

She also heard about the acting company at the John Street Theatre. The Washingtons and the Hamiltons attended frequently and Betsey was most enthusiastic about the evening when the orchestra greeted the President on his entrance by playing a specially composed march. She reported to Theodosia that it was most tuneful and that the President was pleased. The march was "Columbia, the Gem of the Ocean."

These were gay days. The tailors and dressmakers did a flourishing business. Dancing masters were busy teaching new steps and good fiddlers were in demand.

Aaron Burr had been right to move to New York. He was enjoying a most profitable law practice. For the moment he had the field to himself. His strongest rival, Alexander Hamilton, had retired to devote himself to the new and struggling government.

· 15 ·

Finance—
and Politics

The new government had only a foundation—the Constitution. A nation must still be built on it.

The country faced many problems. Washington realized he couldn't cope with all of them. So he chose four advisors. In later years this group of presidential advisors has grown in numbers. It is now called the President's cabinet.

The four men whom Washington chose were

Thomas Jefferson, Secretary of State, to have charge of our relations with other nations; Edmund Randolph, as Attorney General, to advise on legal matters, of which there were many; General Henry Knox, as Secretary of War, because Washington knew we must be ready to defend ourselves; and, of course, Alexander Hamilton as Secretary of the Treasury.

Hamilton's post was the most important of all, for the most serious problems the new nation faced had to do with money matters. Hamilton, who was only thirty-four, was entrusted with solving them.

The United States owed a great deal of money. During the Revolution it had had to borrow heavily from its own citizens and from foreign countries. The states had borrowed, too, and not all of them could pay.

Hamilton knew we would have to clear up this unfavorable situation. A nation that doesn't pay its debts isn't to be trusted any more than a person who doesn't pay his bills.

He knew that he had to take a very bold step, and quickly. So he proposed that instead of many little debts we have one big debt—that we lump all the government owed to other nations and to our own citizens in one big sum and promise to pay this off slowly but surely.

When a government borrows money it gives in return a paper called a bond which is a promise to pay not only what was borrowed but a little extra. This extra amount is called interest. You have lent the government money if you own a United States Bond. Hamilton suggested bonds enough to cover the whole big debt.

There was a great deal of argument about this in Congress and among the citizens. Some people thought it was wrong for the nation to pay up what the states owed. Virginia, for instance, had paid its debts and didn't want to assume the debts of the states that hadn't.

But Hamilton, besides being a statesman, didn't mind being a politician occasionally to achieve a good end. New York had been established as the temporary capital but Congress had to establish a permanent one.

Southerners wanted the new capital to be in the South. Hamilton saw a chance to make a bargain. He proposed that if the Southern congressmen would vote for taking over the state debts he would support the plan for a capital in the South. Finally he won over the influential Jefferson. Virginia voted for the bond plan and our capital went to "the banks of the Potomac," to a new city to be named for the President in a new spot between Virginia and Maryland called the District of Columbia.

This victory for taking over States' debts didn't entirely solve the financial problem. There was the question of "credit." Credit works this way: a man in the grocery business has to have goods on his shelves to sell, but he can't always pay a big amount of cash for the goods. So he borrows either the goods or the money to buy the goods, then repays when he sells the goods.

People have to borrow for various needs. Often governments have to borrow, too. Banks are in business to take your money on deposit and pay you interest on it, then lend it to others at higher interest.

Hamilton had helped start a private bank, the Bank of New York, in 1780. Two other banks followed, one in Philadelphia and one in Baltimore. But they weren't very popular. The average man didn't want anyone else to hold his money for him. He hid it in a mattress or a sugar bowl or buried it under an easily remembered oak tree.

But Hamilton believed in banks and knew a credit system would have to be established to save the new nation. He proposed a national bank, the Bank of the United States, of which the government would own a part and from which it could borrow—within limits. And the government would have the right to inspect the bank's books to see that it was being run correctly.

Most of the stock would be owned by private citizens who would be its officers. It could lend money privately, too, and it could issue paper money.

Many people were for this bank and many against. President Washington was worried, especially by the opposition, which included Jefferson, Madison and Randolph and many congressmen. He asked Hamilton to write out his arguments for, and Jefferson to write out his arguments against it. He read both carefully, then put them in his pocket and rode to Hamilton's house.

Long years later, Betsey recalled:

"I remember the day distinctly. General Washington called at the house looking terribly worried. He shut himself up in the study with my husband for hours. They talked all the time. When he went away he looked much more cheerful. That night my husband did not go to bed at all, but sat up writing, and the next day we had a bank."

Hamilton's answer to the criticism of his plan was so clear that Washington threw his whole-hearted backing to it. Congress finally approved it, and the nation's finances took another step forward.

The government began now to collect some of the money to pay its debts. Congress had, soon after it came into being, established a tariff—a tax on goods brought into the country. To insure against smuggling, Hamilton asked for and got ten small, fast boats to patrol the coast. They were called revenue cutters, and this service grew and grew until it became what we now call the United States Coast Guard.

Now Hamilton added another tax called an excise —a tax on things manufactured and sold in this country.

One of the things on which there was an excise tax was whiskey. Whiskey was made out of corn. Corn was bulky and hard to ship so farmers made their own whiskey. They didn't like the tax. So in Pennsylvania they rebelled. But President Washington was quick to act to support Congress and its taxes. The Whiskey Rebellion was put down. It was a turning point in law and order. The new government gained respect and established authority.

But there were other objections to some of Hamilton's plans. One of the wonderful things about this new nation was that people could disagree, even with the government, and speak their minds.

Something began to happen here that had not happened before. People who favored Hamilton's plans banded together and were known as the Federalists. They became a political party. Those who opposed Hamilton's plans, or some of them at least, chose as their leader Thomas Jefferson and called themselves the Republican party. Ever since then we have had political parties as rivals in our elections. The Federalist party doesn't exist any more and the Republican party of that day later became the Democratic party of today and a new Republican party was formed. These are our major political parties today.

The development of the political party brought Aaron Burr into the national picture in earnest. He had paid so little attention to political issues in those early days that few thought of him in terms of politics.

But Burr could see in the political party a way to power. So the rivalry between Alexander Hamilton and Aaron Burr moved into a new field—moved a little nearer to the river bank in Weehawken.

· 16 ·

The Political
"Boss" Is Born

Once party lines had been drawn on the political front, rivalries—often enmities—began to appear.

The Federalists, because their beliefs had carried the colonies to victory in the Revolution, were the more popular among the voters. But it must be remembered that in those days in most of the states only citizens who owned property could vote and this meant politics was largely in the hands of the wealthy.

This was the side on which Hamilton, if not actually the leader, was very influential.

The Republicans were led by Thomas Jefferson who believed in the rights of the common man. It was he who had written into the Declaration of Independence the words, "all men are created equal."

When President Washington's term drew near its end, the two political parties forgot their differences. Washington was such a good President that both Jefferson and Hamilton urged him to run again. He did and was reëlected. But during his second term the parties drew further apart.

Burr showed little interest in constructive politics. He looked on from the side lines while others built the nation. Busy with this important work, Hamilton did not watch too closely the situation in New York where his father-in-law, Philip Schuyler, was a force.

But in 1791 something happened. Governor Clinton, long an enemy of Hamilton, saw a chance to deal him a blow. Learning that Robert Livingston, a close friend of Hamilton, felt slighted that he had not been appointed Chief Justice of the Supreme Court, Clinton formed an alliance with him. They arranged the nomination of Burr for the Senate against Schuyler.

What's more, they elected him. In the Senate Burr opposed Hamilton's program. Hamilton's dislike of him grew.

"I fear the gentleman is unprincipled both as a public and a private man," he wrote a friend.

Burr went to his duties as senator in Philadelphia, which had become the capital, with a heavy heart. Already the shadow of a serious illness had fallen on his wife. Then, too, his extravagant way of living was catching up with him. He was deeply in debt and his debtors were pressing him.

He returned from Philadelphia as often as possible. He wanted to be with his family. It was necessary now, because of his wife's illness, for him to supervise more closely the younger Theodosia's unusual education. She already was reading Horace and Terence, preparing to begin Homer and Virgil, studying Greek grammar, and discussing philosophy and political economy.

At the age of ten, she spoke German and French, played the pianoforte and harp, skated, rode, and danced. Her mother called her "an intelligent, well-informed girl." For her years she seemed a little more than that!

On May 18, 1794, worn by her long illness, the elder Theodosia died. Burr was disconsolate with grief. Young Theodosia was his only solace now. At eleven, she became the mistress of Richmond Hill, which he had at long last purchased. She entertained her father's guests with great dignity. She was the light of his lonely life.

In his grief Burr had no desire to continue in the Senate. He returned to New York. His debtors were after him again. He had to have money. This time he thought of a scheme which would help him financially and which would also annoy Hamilton.

He and some of his friends chartered the Manhattan Company to provide New York City with a water supply. The law under which the company's charter was issued gave it the right to use its surplus funds "in any other monied transactions or operations not inconsistent with the Constitution and laws of this state or of the United States for the sole benefit of said company."

Burr immediately set the company up in the banking business in rivalry with the Bank of New York, a project dear to Hamilton. There was a loud cry of fraud, but nothing could be done. In later years it became one of New York's largest and most respected banks, The Bank of the Manhattan Company. It still exists today as the Chase Manhattan Bank.

Burr now began to see what could be done by shrewd within-the-law trickery. He took a new look at politics, the field in which power lay.

There was in New York a little organization called the Society of St. Tammany. It was a group composed largely of ex-soldiers, mechanics, laborers, artisans and cartmen. This was not a political organization, because its members couldn't vote. They had no property. Occasionally they took sides in elections—noisily—but without much effect. Their principal quarrel was with the Society of Cincinnati composed of ex-officers only, and of whose New York Chapter Alexander Hamilton was president.

The Society of St. Tammany—its officials called by Indian titles such as Sachem and Sagamore—met in a tavern, drank ale, and spent a good deal of time cursing the rich.

Burr saw possibilities in this organization. He did not join it, but he persuaded some of his friends and co-workers to do so. Soon he was able to dictate the society's moves. But this was of little use to him unless its members could vote.

Burr soon discovered a crafty way to solve this. He found that if several people purchased property together each was granted the vote. He checked the law thoroughly. There was nothing in it to limit the number of people who could buy property together. Soon houses and lots were bought up by many groups of these joint owners—all, oddly enough, members of Tammany. In the next Fifth Ward election there were enough of these votes to elect the Republican candidate.

Burr was on his way to power now. He made a careful list of every voter in the city. He organized ward and precinct meetings. He worked night and day, quietly and effectively.

Too late Hamilton realized what was going on. On the next election day in New York City he rode from poll to poll on a white horse trying to speak to the voters in person. Burr was busy, too, but not on a white horse. He and his men were going from house to house, getting the voters out, providing transportation for them. The Republicans won by a wide margin.

Thus came into being the first political "machine" and the first political "boss," Aaron Burr. The system has come down to us through the years—machine and boss. And Tammany is still with us. From that day to this it has, more often than not, dominated New York City politically.

As Washington approached the end of his second term it became evident that he would not be a candidate again. He believed that no man should serve more than two terms as President. He was tired. His service to the nation had been long and strenuous. He wanted to retire to his beautiful home at Mt. Vernon.

Washington's decision to retire worried Hamilton. He and Jefferson had become bitter political enemies. He did not particularly like John Adams, Washington's Vice-President, but in the end, fearing Jefferson, he supported Adams.

The Federalist party was losing popularity, but it still had enough to elect Adams. However, during his term, trouble developed with both Great Britain and France, who were at war. Each thought we were sending help to the other. They began to seize our ships.

Afraid of trouble developing at home among those taking sides, Congress passed the Sedition Act which limited the right of people to criticize the President and Congress. This weighed heavily against Adams with the people, who did not want their newly won freedom curbed.

The Republicans saw their chance now to break the hold the Federalists had had on the government since its formation. There were no political conventions then as we know them today. Party leaders got together and decided who would be their candidates for President and Vice-President.

Thomas Jefferson, who was extremely popular with the people, was the Republicans' choice to run for President. They knew they must select their Vice-Presidential candidate carefully. New York was growing in population and importance. They needed New York's vote. Governor Clinton was too old, Robert Livingston was of doubtful strength. But Burr— hadn't he maneuvered skillfully to win the last election for the Republicans? They chose Burr.

Hamilton did not like this but he had troubles of his own. He had quarreled openly with Adams. He was so bitter against him that he wrote a scathing pamphlet. It was meant for private circulation, but Burr, who always made it his business to know what was going on, got hold of a copy and made it public.

Now the Federalists divided into factions, each

working against the other. They finally chose Adams for President and C. C. Pinckney of South Carolina for Vice-President. There was talk of defeating Adams by underhand methods and throwing the party strength to Pinckney but Pinckney, a loyal Federalist, refused to allow it.

Voting for the electors wasn't held on one day as now. It took place over several months, for each state voted separately. The tension mounted. Finally South Carolina, Pinckney's own state, voted for Jefferson and Burr. The final count was in—Jefferson 73, Burr 73, Adams 65, Pinckney 64. The Republicans had won.

But who was President? The law said that the candidate obtaining the most electoral votes would be elected President, the one receiving the next highest number, Vice-President.

Jefferson and Burr were tied.

The decision now would rest with the House of Representatives. What could Alexander Hamilton do? The choice for President lay between two men he distrusted.

· 17 ·

Almost
President

Plots and counterplots bubbled and boiled in the political pot in the weeks that followed.

In the eyes of the Federalists, Jefferson with his democratic philosophy was a wild-eyed radical. They saw ruin for the country if he became its leader. There was a definite movement to throw Federalist votes to Burr. Voters knew little of what he stood for because he had not been as active in politics—at least openly.

What they did not know about Burr was, to the conservatives who formed the backbone of the Federalist party, better than what they did know about Jefferson.

Hamilton, who had planned to retire from politics, was back in it now with a vengeance. He had been a bitter opponent of Jefferson, but his feeling about Burr was more than just opposition. It was hatred. He had worked with Jefferson in the cabinet. He knew his love of the country and that he placed country above self. Much as he disliked Jefferson, he had to place him above Burr.

"If there be a man in the world I ought to hate, it is Jefferson," he wrote Gouverneur Morris, "but the public good must be paramount to every private consideration."

As time grew closer for Congress to meet and vote on the issue, Hamilton's letters became more vitriolic, more reckless, even more irresponsible.

In one to Oliver Wolcott, former Secretary of the Treasury, he referred to Burr "whose private character is not defended by his most partial friends. He is bankrupt beyond redemption, except by the plunder of his country. If he can he will certainly disturb our institutions to secure to himself permanent power and with it wealth."

But Hamilton's influence was beginning to wane. The Federalists wanted anyone but Jefferson. They openly plotted to elect Burr. They even went so far as to send an emissary to him in New York where he was busy with the impending marriage of his beloved daughter, Theodosia. They promised to throw enough votes to him for victory over Jefferson if he would promise them certain things.

It is to Burr's credit that he refused. Some say he felt certain of victory; others, that it was an honest stand. But he would make no commitment of any kind.

Came the long-awaited meeting of the House of Representatives. Its members assembled in Washington, the new capital. It was just half a city, unfinished, not yet beautiful; the streets full of mud holes. Its boarding house—it had no hotel—was crowded.

The city was tense—the whole nation was tense—as the members trudged through a heavy snowstorm to the meeting.

The voting was by states. Members could vote individually, but a majority vote decided the state's ballot. And a majority of states was required for election. The first ballot was taken. New Jersey, Pennsylvania, New York, Virginia, North Carolina, Kentucky, Tennessee and Georgia voted for Jefferson. Massachusetts, Rhode Island, New Hampshire, Connecticut, Delaware and South Carolina voted for Burr. Vermont and Maryland—their members tied—voted blank. It was eight for Jefferson, six for Burr. A majority was nine. Neither candidate had won.

But the vote of the individual members was fifty-five for Burr, fifty-one for Jefferson. If it had not been for the state rule, Burr would have been President.

All night the voting went on, each ballot the same. Outside, the snowstorm raged. Joseph Nicholson, representative from Maryland, ill with a fever, had dragged himself to the House in order to take part in the voting. Another representative, viewing him on a crude cot in the cold and draughty room, wrote his wife, "It is a chance that this kills him. I would not thus expose myself for any President on earth."

Now and then the representatives were allowed a few hours sleep—if they could sleep on a straight-backed chair or curled up on the floor. For five days, from early morning until well into the night, the balloting continued with no change. Any one of six men, changing his vote, would have elected Jefferson; any one of three could have turned the tide for Burr.

On the sixth day, the break came. The Maryland and Vermont delegations had been tied. The Burr delegates from each state decided the struggle must end. They would not vote for Jefferson but they did refrain from voting for Burr. They cast blank ballots, thus giving their delegations' majority vote to Jefferson. Once this had happened the delegations from Delaware and South Carolina, which had been for Burr, refrained from voting entirely.

The tally thus was: Jefferson, 10 states; Burr, 4; not voting 2.

The election was over but not the bitterness. Jefferson was President. Burr was Vice-President. But Jefferson knew Burr's strength now. He wanted no close rival. He joined Burr's enemies. Hamilton, no longer politically important himself, joined those who were out to crush his old rival. Events were closing in on the feud.

· 18 ·

"Despicable"

The victory of Jefferson was an empty one for Hamilton. To him the successful candidate was just the lesser of two evils.

"We are all Republicans—we are all Federalists," Jefferson said in his inaugural address and proceeded to be a very fine President. However, Hamilton was unhappy. His political career was really over but he did not know it.

In 1801 he helped found the New York *Evening Post* to give the waning Federalist party a faint voice in an increasingly Republican nation. His pen flashed occasionally in its columns. It is still published today —the oldest newspaper in America.

Along with political adversity, personal tragedy entered his life. His hope lay in his eldest son Philip, nineteen, a graduate of King's College, who seemed on the verge of a brilliant career.

On a November evening in 1801, Philip and an-

Eacker angrily challenged the young men to a duel.

other young man occupied a box at the theatre. In the next box sat George Eacker, a Republican, who in a Fourth of July speech had attacked the elder Hamilton. Philip and his friend made disparaging remarks about Eacker loud enough for him to hear. He challenged each of them to a duel.

Dueling was against the law but it was not uncommon. It was considered the gentleman's way of defending his honor. Seldom were the duels fatal. Occasionally there was a slight wound, more often not even that.

Eacker met Philip's friend on the field of honor at Paulus Hook. They exchanged several shots, missed, and called it off. It was Philip's turn on November 23rd. This time Eacker's first bullet found its mark. Philip fell and, a few days later, died.

The grief in the Hamilton family was to bring another tragedy. Hamilton and Betsey were inconsolable, but Angelica, Philip's sister, was so stricken with shock that she became insane.

Hamilton a few months before had begun building a new home on fifteen acres of hilltop land, far northeast of the growing city. It had a magnificent view of both the Hudson River and the East River.

The bereaved Hamilton devoted much of his time now to its completion. The family moved into it in 1802. It was a large house, two stories high, with verandas north and south. He planted thirteen gum trees to symbolize the thirteen original states.

Hamilton rode ten miles to his office each day. He still prospered as a lawyer, but he spent much time in his home, which in memory of his Scottish forebears he called "The Grange."

"A garden, you know," he wrote to C. C. Pinckney, "is a very useful refuge of a disappointed politician."

Meantime Burr was a busy and, according to all accounts, a brilliant Vice-President in Washington. But he was unhappy, too. Jefferson, fearing Burr's obvious political skill and potential strength, steered clear of him. So did most Republican leaders. He was never consulted on any questions of policy.

His beloved Theodosia had borne him a grandson, Aaron Burr Alston. But the event had left her an invalid. Burr himself took her to Saratoga Springs and Ballston Spa, but to no avail. Still ill, she returned to South Carolina.

Burr was the loneliest man in Washington. Disliked by the leaders of his own party even more than by those of the opposition, he had lost all national standing. But he still had a certain power in New York City, the power of the "machine" he had built up.

An election for governor of New York was coming up. Early in 1804 Burr had himself nominated for the post. Governor Clinton controlled the upstate Republicans and they nominated Morgan Lewis, Chief Justice of the State Supreme Court. Two Republicans were running against each other.

The Federalists were desperate. There was often talk of supporting Burr. Indeed the Federalists were desperate not only in New York but in national politics, too. Some of the die-hards—mostly the New England conservatives—now concocted a plot whereby the New England states would secede and form a nation of their own.

For this they needed the power and financial strength of New York. The plotters turned to Burr. They knew he had been frozen out of his own party. They met with him secretly and offered him their plan.

There is no indication that Burr agreed to it. But he did want Federalist support for the governorship. So he avoided a definite answer.

Hamilton was in a fury when he heard of the plot.

He was always willing to believe anything of Burr. In a blind rage he lashed out at his old enemy. He wrote letters and he made speeches.

At a dinner party at the home of Judge John Taylor in Albany, he was particularly bitter. One of the guests, Dr. Charles D. Cooper, agreeing, thought some of the things he said should be passed along as campaign material.

To one friend, Dr. Cooper wrote:

"General Hamilton has come out decidedly against Burr; indeed, when he was here he spoke of him as a dangerous man and ought not to be trusted."

To another:

"General Hamilton and Judge Kent have declared in substance that they look upon Mr. Burr as a dangerous man, and one who ought not to be trusted with the reins of government. . . . I could detail to you a still more despicable opinion which General Hamilton had expressed of Mr. Burr."

The letters were printed in the Albany *Register*. Aaron Burr clipped them and put them in his desk.

The campaign became hotter and hotter. Then came the election. When the votes were counted, Burr had received 22,139 and Lewis 30,829. Burr had lost more than the governorship. He was still Vice-

President but his political career was at an end. Hamilton retired again to his Grange.

On the night of June 18, 1804, Hamilton was in his study. There came a knock at the door. He answered it himself. It was William Van Ness, a friend of Aaron Burr. He handed Hamilton an envelope. Hamilton tore it open. Inside was a letter. He read:

SIR,

I send for your perusal a letter signed Charles D. Cooper, which, though apparently published some time ago, has but very recently come to my knowledge. Mr. Van Ness, who does me the favour to deliver this, will point out to you that clause of the letter to which I particularly request your attention. You must perceive, sir, the necessity of a prompt and unqualified acknowledgment or denial of the use of any expressions which would warrant the assertions of Mr. Cooper. I have the honour to be

Your obedient servant,

A. BURR

Hamilton stared at the letter. There were two newspaper clippings. He did not need to read them. A glance told him what they were.

Hamilton stared at the letter.

There was a moment of silence. Then Hamilton spoke.

"This matter requires consideration," he said. "I will send a reply shortly."

Van Ness bowed and left. Alexander Hamilton stood there with the letter—and his fate—in his hands.

· 19 ·

The

Challenge

The situation, as Hamilton said, did indeed call for consideration. If he admitted expressing a "despicable opinion" Burr might well challenge him to a duel. If he denied he had done so, Dr. Cooper might consider himself represented as a liar.

There was a middle choice which might have saved the day. Hamilton could have explained that what one man might consider "despicable" another might not. What he had said might be despicable only in Dr. Cooper's opinion. Burr would have had to accept that explanation.

But Hamilton would not take that course. After two days, he wrote a rambling and uncertain letter. He pleaded he was just using political language. Burr quickly rejected the excuse and demanded that Hamilton disavow anything he had said "derogatory to my honor." Hamilton again tried to dodge a definite reply. Burr, tired of evasion, now delivered a formal challenge to a duel. Too late, Hamilton answered that what Dr. Cooper had heard "did not attribute to Colonel Burr any instance of dishonorable conduct."

But things had gone too far. Burr repeated his challenge. Van Ness, his friend, delivered it in person. Nathaniel Pendleton, who had been acting for Hamilton in the negotiations, accepted it on June 27th, 1804.

Pistols at ten paces—the date, July 11th; the place, the plateau of Weehawken across the Hudson River from New York!

Two of the nation's leading figures—one its Vice-

President, the other its former Secretary of the Treasury—were to meet in mortal combat. And yet it was kept a complete secret for two weeks.

On June 23rd, Burr celebrated Theo's birthday, even though Theo was hundreds of miles away. He gave a party at Richmond Hill. He and his guests "laughed an hour and danced an hour" and drank her health.

On July 4th, the Society of the Cincinnati held its annual meeting in Fraunces Tavern. Hamilton and Burr were both there. Hamilton, president of the organization, was unusually gay that evening. At a request from fellow members that he sing an old favorite, "The Drum," he readily agreed, and, head thrown back, and smiling, he obliged.

> *We're going to war and when we die,*
> *We'll want a man of God nearby.*

Two seats from him Burr rested his head on his hand, elbow on table. He never took his eyes off the entertainer. His expression was thoughtful—even grave. Applause and shouts followed the song. When things quieted down again, the members noticed that Burr's chair was empty.

Each man made his will and set in order his affairs. Each wrote letters to the one he loved best.

"I am indebted to you, my dearest Theodosia," Burr wrote to his daughter, "for a very great portion of the happiness which I have enjoyed in this life. You have completely satisfied all that my heart and affections had hoped or even wished. With a little more perseverance, determination and industry, you will obtain all that my ambition or vanity had fondly imagined. Let your son have occasion to be proud that he had a mother. Adieu!"

Hamilton wrote two letters to his wife. The first read:

"This letter, my dear Eliza, will not be delivered to you, unless I shall first have terminated my earthly career, to begin, as I humbly hope, from redeeming grace and divine mercy, a happy immortality. If it had been possible for me to have avoided the interview, my love for you and my precious children would have been alone a decisive motive. But it was not possible without sacrifices which would have rendered me unworthy of your esteem. I need not tell you of the pangs I feel from the idea of quitting you, and exposing you to the anguish I know you would feel. Nor could I dwell on the topic, lest it should unman me. The consolations of religion, my beloved, can alone support you; and these you have a right to enjoy. Fly to the bosom of your God, and be comforted. With my last idea I shall cherish the sweet hope of meeting you in a better world. Adieu, best of wives—best of women. Embrace all my darling children for me."

The night before the duel, Hamilton kissed Betsey good night and with heavy heart watched her climb the stairs. His excuse of work had aroused no suspicion in her trusting mind.

Hamilton entered the library and closed the door. He lit the candle on his desk. He must make this clear to Betsey or she would never understand why he had undertaken the duel. He sat down and carefully dipped his quill in the ink.

". . . The scruples of a Christian have determined me to expose my own life to any extent, rather than subject myself to the guilt of taking the life of another. This much increases my hazards, and redoubles my pangs for you. But you had rather I should die innocent than live guilty. Heaven can preserve me, and I humbly hope will; but, in the contrary event,

I charge you to remember that you are a Christian. God's will be done! The will of a merciful God must be good. Once more,

Adieu, my darling, darling wife. . . ."

No one knows what Aaron Burr was thinking that sultry July night.

· 20 ·

"This Is
a Mortal Wound"

The morning of July 11th was humid, a heat haze
hanging over the city. Across the Hudson River lay
Weehawken Heights, not far from Hoboken, a steep
rocky elevation covered with small trees and tangled
bushes.

Below the heights, not more than twenty feet above
the water, was a grassy, shelflike ledge about six feet
wide. It was inaccessible except at low tide. Every-

thing had been done to keep the duel from becoming known. The secluded solitude of this spot—barely room for the ten paces—helped keep the secret.

At daybreak John Swarthout, a friend, had called for Burr and found him sleeping peacefully. He awakened him. William Van Ness, his second, soon joined them. They rowed with muffled oars to the Jersey shore and climbed to the heights.

It was 6:30 when they arrived and the sun was now out. They removed their coats and began to clear the ledge, breaking off branches that protruded from the bushes and trees.

A few minutes before seven another boat touched the rocks below. Hamilton and his second, Nathaniel Pendleton, stepped out. A third man remained in the boat, along with the boatman. He was Dr. David Hosack.

Hamilton and Burr nodded formally to each other, their seconds proceeding immediately with the usual preparations. They measured ten paces. Pendleton, for Hamilton, won the first toss—choice of place. He chose the upper portion. He won the second toss, too. He was to give the word "present" at which each was to fire.

The duelists took their places. Hamilton looked out over the river to the city which he had helped start toward greatness. Pendleton handed him his pistol.

"Will you have the hairspring set?" he asked.

"Not this time," was the reply.

There was a moment's silence.

"Are you ready?" Pendleton asked.

"Yes," said two voices.

Not even a leaf stirred.

"Present!" said Pendleton.

A shot rang out. In the time it takes a heart to beat Hamilton rose convulsively on his toes. A second shot rang out, this one from Hamilton's pistol, thrown upward by his movement. It clipped a few leaves from the tree above which fell as Hamilton himself pitched forward on his face.

As his adversary fell, Burr stepped forward as if to go to his aid. Already Dr. Hosack and the boatman, hearing the shots, were scurrying up the rocks. Van Ness raised an umbrella to hide Burr's face and quickly led him down the sharp path to his boat.

When Dr. Hosack reached Hamilton's side he was sitting up, Pendleton's arm about him.

"This is a mortal wound, doctor," Hamilton said and slumped.

He was carried to the boat. Once he regained consciousness for a moment.

"Take care of the pistol," he said feebly. "It may go off and do harm. Pendleton knows that I did not intend to fire at him."

He was taken to the home of William Bayard on Jane Street.

"Let Mrs. Hamilton be sent for," he said. "Let the event be gradually broken to her, but give her hope."

Betsey, who had not even suspected the duel was

to be held, hurried to his side with the children. Many of his friends gathered, too. Other doctors were called in, including surgeons from a French frigate in the harbor near by. For thirty-two hours Hamilton lay suffering.

At two o'clock on July 12th, he reached out his hand.

"My beloved wife——" he said, and his heart stopped beating.

· 21 ·

A Vice-President
in Hiding

An entire nation mourned Alexander Hamilton.

Newspapers vied with each other in expressions of sorrow. Sermons were preached in every church. Mass meetings were held in many cities. Flags were at half-mast. Everyone in public life spoke his sorrow.

Even his greatest enemy within his own party, John Adams, said:

"No one wanted to get rid of Alexander Hamilton *that* way!"

His funeral on July 14th was attended by great and small. The Mayor, the City Council, members of Congress, foreign ministers, the Cincinnati and Tammany, friends and foes, marched to muffled drumbeat through silent crowds lining the streets. He was buried in Trinity Churchyard. A pall hung over the city and the nation for many days.

Aaron Burr was nowhere to be seen in all of this. From the Weehawken shore he had gone into hiding. When a coroner's jury indicted him for murder, friends spirited him away to Philadelphia. When a New Jersey jury followed suit he slipped out of the city and made his way under the name of R. King to Georgia. From there he wrote his beloved Theodosia:

"You have doubtless heard that there has subsisted for some time a contention of a very singular nature between the two states of New York and New Jersey. . . . The subject in dispute is which shall have the honor of hanging the Vice-President."

He was still Vice-President of the United States— the first and last Vice-President ever accused of murder!

· 22 ·

"Treason!"

Burr did not need to hide when he reached the South, for there was little feeling against him there. Indeed, when the storm had blown over and the furor had subsided, he started north and was greeted at Savannah by a brass band and a large crowd of cheering citizens.

After all, he was still Vice-President, and so when the Senate met again on November 5, 1804, Burr had returned to Washington and was in the chair. He finished his term with great dignity. The following March he entered the Senate for the last time. The room was hushed as he rose to make his farewell.

"This House, I need not remind you, is a sanctuary; a citadel of law, of order, and of liberty. And it is here . . . will resistance be made to the storms of political frenzy and the silent arts of corruption—and if the Constitution be destined ever to perish . . . which God avert, its expiring agonies will be witnessed on this floor."

He bowed. Then, descending from his chair, he walked out, erect and alone. The door slammed behind him.

The scene was reported in the Washington *Federalist* the next morning.

"It is said to be the most dignified, sublime and impressive speech that ever was uttered. The whole Senate was in tears."

This would have been the ideal time for Burr to retire from the political scene. The charge of murder was all but forgotten. He had regained a certain respect. He could have gone quietly back to the practice of law, at which he was brilliant, and lived happily, and comfortably, ever after.

However, by this time the man had become a schemer. He was not content to live the quiet life even if he could do so successfully. He longed for fame and power, as well as fortune. And a situation had developed which seemed to give him the opportunity for all three.

During Jefferson's administration an old difficulty had been cleared up. Spain had long owned Florida to the southeast, and Louisiana to the west of the States. There had been trouble on these borders. There was even more now that our pioneers were expanding westward. There was constant friction.

Now suddenly it became known that France had acquired Florida and Louisiana from Spain by a secret treaty. Napoleon, the man on horseback, was looming large. There seemed little doubt that he planned to conquer all of Europe. What if he decided to take over America, too? He now had a big foothold.

President Jefferson was a pacifist. He did not want war with anyone. But the nation needed room. It needed the port of New Orleans for trade transportation.

He had one hope. Perhaps France would sell us New Orleans and Florida. It was worth trying. He asked Napoleon to name a price. The offer was made at the right time. Napoleon was in difficulties, and he needed money. He set a price of $15,000,000, and along with New Orleans he would throw in all of Louisiana. No one knew how big this territory was. It turned out to be enormous and this was probably the greatest real estate bargain in history.

Spain protested the sale. It had hoped by selling Louisiana to France to set up an in-between territory to separate the growing United States and the rich Mexico.

Even before his term as Vice-President was over, Burr's eyes had turned toward Mexico. Colonel James Wilkinson, with whom he had fought at Quebec and who was now one of the American commissioners of Louisiana Territory, had unfolded a lavish scheme to him. It was a scheme for stirring up revolt against Spain in Mexico and cashing in on it.

Burr was attracted by anything that would restore his fortunes and political power. Even if the plan concerning Mexico did not go through, there was money to be made in land speculation. The states must expand.

The plots and counterplots that resulted were many and complicated. Burr and his friends—and some of these were important, including senators and even Andrew Jackson at one time—tried to get help from England as well as France. They even bought almost half a million acres of land in Louisiana.

It seemed certain that the United States must go to war with Spain over the border of the newly acquired territory. This would be the time for the conspirators to strike at Mexico. But Spain, after much blustering and even an invasion, backed down. War talk quieted.

It was too late for Burr to give up his ambitious plans. He was gathering a following of adventurous men for his expedition. He had ordered boats to take them down the Ohio and the Mississippi.

His headquarters were on an island in the Ohio River owned by Harman Blennerhassett, one of his financial backers. It was from here that the expedition was to set out. Blennerhassett undoubtedly had visions of the conquest of Mexico.

The enterprise was doomed from the start. Burr and his colleagues never obtained enough money for a real expedition. And Burr did not know that his co-leader, Colonel Wilkinson, had long been in the pay of the Spanish even while Governor of Louisiana.

When the straggling expedition set out, and Burr's enemies began to dog his footsteps, Wilkinson turned against him, probably to save his own hide.

The Spanish, with a great network of spies in the states, were the first to spread reports that Burr's plan was to form a new nation, taking some of the western territories and even states with him.

Wilkinson now seized on this and, getting a letter in code from Burr, changed it enough to indicate that the reports were true.

President Jefferson, long Burr's enemy, saw a chance to crush him. He issued a proclamation denouncing this "military expedition against the dominions of Spain." There was no accusation of treason in the proclamation. But, coupled with the rumors the Spanish had spread, this was the impression given.

The whole country, inflamed by the reports, turned against Burr. Blennerhassett's island was raided by militia men. But Burr was not there. He was proceeding quietly down the Mississippi with his little band in unarmed houseboats. There were fifty-five men, a few women and children and some Negro servants. It scarcely seemed to be an expedition to form a new nation!

The alarm had been sounded. Army detachments, the militia, and even government gunboats were sent out to capture this "dangerous" band.

On January 10th, when he and his small flotilla halted at Bayou Pierre, Burr learned for the first time of the tumult his enterprise had caused and of the fact that military expeditions were moving against him. He surrendered to civil authorities, hoping to clear himself in court. But the determination of his enemies to ruin him was so strong that friends advised him to go into hiding.

He fled into the wilderness. Immediately a $2,000 reward was offered for his capture. A few nights later he stopped at a cabin to ask directions to an inn. The resident, Nicholas Perkins, recognized under the homespun farmer's pantaloons a pair of sleek city

Burr sent a letter in code to Wilkinson.

boots. Looking up, he saw the keen sharp eyes.

When the inquirer, having been given directions, left, Perkins turned to his companion.

"That," he said, "is Aaron Burr."

The next day Burr was under arrest—charged with treason.

· 23 ·

The
Last Days

Fate pursued Burr rapidly now. President Jefferson seemed determined to destroy him completely. All the rumors of treachery and treason centered on the slight, elegantly dressed figure who seemed destined to hang from a gallows.

However, the founding fathers had made the laws of the new nation well. In spite of everything, Burr must have a trial by jury.

It took place in Richmond, Virginia, starting in August, 1807, with Chief Justice John Marshall presiding.

Day after day witnesses took the stand. Few, however, had any direct evidence to give. They told of things they had heard, of things they had supposed or guessed, of things that "appeared to be." At no time did they pin Burr down to any actual "overt" act.

There was no proof that he had been present when any move had been made that could be held traitorous. All evidence pointed to the fact that, on the night of December 10th, Burr had been far away from the place where the prosecution contended "acts of war" were taking place.

Burr's lawyers, tired of these accusations, moved that further testimony be stopped. There were days of arguments. The prosecution could not promise to bring in anything more direct than it had offered. Justice Marshall decided that the case must go to the jury.

The verdict came almost immediately.

"Not guilty!"

Burr was free—but his enemies would not give up.

They tried to renew the charges. His creditors swooped down on him. He lost the lands he had bought. In Baltimore a crowd threatened to "string him up." He fled to Philadelphia and hid in an obscure French boarding house.

At the age of fifty-one, Burr looked upon the ruins of his life. Bankrupt, hounded by creditors, afraid to show his face—where could he turn?

He thought of Europe. But even to flee the country which seemed now to hate him required stealth. He booked passage on a British packet under another name. On June 7, 1807, a muffler over his face, he slipped aboard. Theo, heavily veiled, said a tearful farewell, and he sailed.

He landed in England and for a time was able to forget what lay behind. He was taken up socially and earned his way with his wit and charm. But British official circles were not too friendly. Spain was now a British ally and could not be offended. And the American ministry reflected President Jefferson's cool enmity. Eventually he was made to feel it best that he quit England. He moved on to Sweden, Denmark, then France.

He tried to reach Napoleon with new schemes concerning Mexico, but everyone was afraid to deal with him now. Theo fell ill in America. He felt he must get back to her. He sold clothes, books, even the little presents he had bought for his grandson.

Under an assumed name and hiding behind a black beard he sailed for America. He landed in Boston with no one to greet him. He made his way secretly back to New York, still afraid to show his face.

But he could not hide all his life. What would happen if people knew he had returned? He decided to find out. He let a simple item be published in a newspaper.

"Aaron Burr," it said, "has returned to the city and has resumed the practice of law at 9 Nassau Street."

It had an amazing result. Hundreds sought out the tiny office on Nassau Street with its little tin sign. Among these were few friends—but many admirers of his ability as a lawyer. Within two weeks he took in $2,000 in fees. At least his fortunes had taken a good turn.

But tragedy was not finished with him. Theo wrote that his grandson had died. Burr sent a messenger to bring his beloved daughter to New York. She sailed from Charleston on December 13, 1812, on the pilot boat *Patriot*. The next night there was a terrific gale. The *Patriot* vanished completely. Everything for which Burr had to live vanished with it. He haunted the docks for weeks in the hope he could sight the *Patriot's* sail. It was never heard from again.

Life went on. He was seldom invited anywhere socially. Politically, no party wanted him, no candidate would accept his support. He was the first to realize the presidential possibilities of General Andrew Jackson, but when the General became head of the nation, Burr received no reward.

He never forgot the dream of the Southwest and when Texas, under the leadership of American settlers, won its independence, he exclaimed:

"I was right. What was treason in me thirty years ago is patriotism now."

On July 3, 1833, New York was astounded by the announcement that he had married Mme. Eliza Jumel. Widow of Stephen Jumel, she was the wealthiest woman in town. He was 77, and she was 58.

Mme. Jumel was his match for she had no more social standing than he—an adventuress who reportedly had married M. Jumel, a rich merchant, for his money.

The marriage to Burr was short-lived, she suing for divorce.

There wasn't much left now for Aaron Burr. Shortly afterward he suffered a stroke, then another. He continued to receive clients—propped up in bed. His body was weak but his mind still keen. He loved to talk of the old days, the days when he and Hamilton were young rivals.

One of his frequent visitors was a neighboring schoolboy, who liked just to sit at his feet even when Burr was too tired and worn to talk. On one of these visits he found Burr reading Laurence Sterne's *Tristram Shandy,* a wise and witty book. Burr finished the book, put it down, and smiled down on the youngster.

"Perhaps," he said, almost to himself, "if I had read this earlier I might have thought the world wide enough for Alexander Hamilton and me."

On September 14, 1836, Aaron Burr died. He was a belated, but just as certainly as Alexander Hamilton, victim of the most famous duel in American history.

Landmarks

History has a way of coming alive if you can see the actual places where events took place, or look on things which belonged to the people involved. For that reason we include this list of places and things concerning Alexander Hamilton and Aaron Burr.

In Charlestown, on the island of Nevis in the West Indies, there is a crumbling wall which is said to be all that remains of the birthplace of Alexander Hamilton. Its authenticity is doubtful. For many years it was recorded in histories and biographies that Hamilton was born on January 11, 1757. However, in recent years documents have been found which establish his birthdate as January 11, 1755.

The Grange, Hamilton's home, is at 287 Convent Avenue, New York City. It can be seen daily 10:00 A.M. to 5:00 P.M.; Saturdays, 10:00 A.M. to 1:00 P.M.

Hamilton's grave is in Trinity Churchyard, Broadway and Wall Street, New York City.

Burr's grave is at Princeton University.

"The Fields," where Hamilton addressed his first crowd, is now City Hall Park, New York City.

St. Paul's Chapel, where Hamilton went to church, is at Broadway and Vesey Street, New York City.

The Schuyler Mansion, at Clinton and Catherine Streets, Albany, New York, is where Hamilton and Elizabeth Schuyler were married. It is open to the public, 9:00 A.M. to 5:00 P.M. daily, and on Sundays, 1:00 P.M. to 5:00 P.M.

Federal Hall has been replaced by the Sub-Treasury

Building at Wall and Broad Streets, but a tablet marks the spot where President Washington took the oath of office, and a fine museum holds many relics of the times. It was at Federal Hall that Hamilton became Secretary of the Treasury. His first home in New York was right across the street.

Fraunces Tavern, at Broad and Pearl Streets, New York City, is where Washington made his farewell address to his officers, and where the dinner of the Sons of Cincinnati was held just seven days before the Hamilton-Burr duel. This restaurant is open for lunch and dinner.

Independence Hall, Philadelphia, is where Hamilton and fifty-four other patriots fought for the Constitution of the United States.

Yorktown Battlefield can be seen at Yorktown, Virginia. The British redoubts are still standing, and some of the American redoubts—including the one which Hamilton commanded—have been reconstructed.

A plaque and a stone mark the spot where the duel was fought on the shores of Weehawken. It can be reached from New York City by going through the Lincoln Tunnel, following Eastern Boulevard, turning right off Eastern Boulevard at the traffic light at the top of a steep hill, and going four short blocks to Hamilton Avenue. There a fenced-in area contains the stone on which Hamilton's head rested when he was mortally wounded.

The dueling pistols used by Hamilton and Burr are owned by the Chase Manhattan Bank of New York City. They are not on display but from time to time the Bank permits them to be exhibited in various cities over the country.

Trumbull's portrait of Hamilton hangs in the Governor's Room in New York's City Hall. An excellent engraving of him may be obtained for ten dollars. It is on the ten-dollar bill!

Index